D1548565

This is a gem of a book, laced with clinical wisdom. Not only is it valuable for novice supervisors, but experienced supervisors will find a treasure trove of nuggets to enhance their practice. It's relatively brief as well—a remarkable combination of qualities to meet the needs of busy practitioners.
—**James Bennett-Levy, PhD,** Professor in Mental Health, University Centre for Rural Health (North Coast), University of Sydney, Lismore, Australia

This thoughtfully written book offers pragmatic and informative guidance for individuals striving to become competent and effective cognitive–behavioral therapy supervisors. Written in conversational terms by two well-respected experts in this supervisory model, this resource elucidates an approach for creating a respectful, safe, and collaborative supervisory climate. It is within such an environment that the cognitive–behavioral supervisory methods and techniques so clearly portrayed can best be utilized and can enhance supervisees' learning and the quality of care they provide.
—**Nadine J. Kaslow, PhD, ABPP,** Emory University School of Medicine and 2014 President of the American Psychological Association

This text is a rare achievement. In a lean yet robust way, Newman and Kaplan communicate essential elements and nuanced supervisory processes. Through concise explanations, vivid examples, and illustrative dialogues, the authors succeed mightily in providing a valuable resource for training the next generation of cognitive–behavioral therapists.
—**Robert D. Friedberg, PhD, ABPP, ACT,** Professor; Director, Center for the Study and Treatment of Anxious Youth at Palo Alto University, Palo Alto, CA

Supervision Essentials for

Cognitive–
Behavioral
Therapy

Clinical Supervision
Essentials Series

CLINICAL SUPERVISION ESSENTIALS

HANNA LEVENSON *and* ARPANA G. INMAN, Series Editors

Supervision Essentials for

Cognitive–
Behavioral
Therapy

Cory F. Newman and Danielle A. Kaplan

American Psychological Association • Washington, DC

Published by
American Psychological Association
750 First Street, NE
Washington, DC 20002
www.apa.org

To order
APA Order Department
P.O. Box 92984
Washington, DC 20090-2984
Tel: (800) 374-2721; Direct: (202) 336-5510
Fax: (202) 336-5502; TDD/TTY: (202) 336-6123
Online: www.apa.org/pubs/books
E-mail: order@apa.org

In the U.K., Europe, Africa, and the Middle East, copies may be ordered from
American Psychological Association
3 Henrietta Street
Covent Garden, London
WC2E 8LU England

Typeset in Minion by Circle Graphics, Inc., Columbia, MD

Printer: United Book Press, Inc., Baltimore, MD
Cover Designer: Mercury Publishing Services, Inc., Rockville, MD

The opinions and statements published are the responsibility of the authors, and such opinions and statements do not necessarily represent the policies of the American Psychological Association.

Library of Congress Cataloging-in-Publication Data

Names: Newman, Cory Frank, author. | Kaplan, Danielle Alissa, author.
Title: Supervision essentials for cognitive-behavioral therapy /
  Cory F. Newman and Danielle A. Kaplan.
Description: Washington, DC : American Psychological Association, 2016. |
  Includes bibliographical references and index.
Identifiers: LCCN 2015050646 | ISBN 9781433822797 | ISBN 1433822792
Subjects: LCSH: Cognitive therapy—Study and teaching—Supervision. |
  Psychotherapists—Supervision of.
Classification: LCC RC489.C63 N494 2016 | DDC 616.89/1425—dc23
LC record available at http://lccn.loc.gov/2015050646

British Library Cataloguing-in-Publication Data
A CIP record is available from the British Library.

Printed in the United States of America
First Edition

http://dx.doi.org/10.1037/14950-000

To Norman and Phyllis Newman, my father and mother,
and my original "supervisors," with love and gratitude.
—*Cory F. Newman*

To Alan, Jonathan, and Annalise,
with the happiest part of my heart.
—*Danielle A. Kaplan*

Contents

Foreword to the Clinical Supervision Essentials Series

W e are both clinical supervisors. We teach courses on supervision of students who are in training to become therapists. We give workshops on supervision and consult with supervisors about their supervision practices. We write and do research on the topic. To say we eat and breathe supervision might be a little exaggerated, but only slightly. We are fully invested in the field and in helping supervisors provide the most informed and helpful guidance to those learning the profession. We also are committed to helping supervisees/consultees/trainees become better collaborators in the supervisory endeavor by understanding their responsibilities in the supervisory process.

What is supervision? Supervision is critical to the practice of therapy. As stated by Edward Watkins[1] in the *Handbook of Psychotherapy Supervision*, "Without the enterprise of psychotherapy supervision, . . . the practice of psychotherapy would become highly suspect and would or should cease to exist" (p. 603).

Supervision has been defined as

> an intervention provided by a more senior member of a profession to a more junior colleague or colleagues who typically (but not always) are members of that same profession. This relationship
>
> - is evaluative and hierarchical,
> - extends over time, and

---

[1] Watkins, C. E., Jr. (Ed.). (1997). *Handbook of psychotherapy supervision*. New York, NY: Wiley.

- has the simultaneous purposes of enhancing the professional functioning of the more junior person(s); monitoring the quality of professional services offered to the clients that she, he, or they see; and serving as a gatekeeper for the particular profession the supervisee seeks to enter. (p. 9)[2]

It is now widely acknowledged in the literature that supervision is a "distinct activity" in its own right.[3] One cannot assume that being an excellent therapist generalizes to being an outstanding supervisor. Nor can one imagine that good supervisors can just be "instructed" in how to supervise through purely academic, didactic means.

So how does one become a good supervisor?

Supervision is now recognized as a core competency domain for psychologists[4,5] and other mental health professionals. Guidelines have been created to facilitate the provision of competent supervision across professional groups and internationally (e.g., American Psychological Association,[6] American Association of Marriage and Family Therapy,[7] British Psychological Society,[8,9] Canadian Psychological Association[10]).

---

[2] Bernard, J. M., & Goodyear, R. K. (2014). *Fundamentals of clinical supervision* (5th ed.). Boston, MA: Pearson.

[3] Bernard, J. M., & Goodyear, R. K. (2014). *Fundamentals of clinical supervision* (5th ed.). Boston, MA: Pearson.

[4] Fouad, N., Grus, C. L., Hatcher, R. L., Kaslow, N. J., Hutchings, P. S., Madson, M. B., ... Crossman, R. E. (2009). Competency benchmarks: A model for understanding and measuring competence in professional psychology across training levels. *Training and Education in Professional Psychology, 3*(4 Suppl.), S5–S26. http://dx.doi.org/10.1037/a0015832

[5] Kaslow, N. J., Rubin, N. J., Bebeau, M. J., Leigh, I. W., Lichtenberg, J. W., Nelson, P. D., ... Smith, I. L. (2007). Guiding principles and recommendations for the assessment of competence. *Professional Psychology: Research and Practice, 38*, 441–51. http://dx.doi.org/10.1037/0735-7028.38.5.441

[6] American Psychological Association. (2014). *Guidelines for clinical supervision in health service psychology.* Retrieved from http://www.apa.org/about/policy/guidelines-supervision.pdf

[7] American Association of Marriage and Family Therapy. (2007). *AAMFT approved supervisor designation standards and responsibilities handbook.* Retrieved from http://www.aamft.org/imis15/Documents/Approved_Supervisor_handbook.pdf

[8] British Psychological Society. (2003). *Policy guidelines on supervision in the practice of clinical psychology.* Retrieved from http://www.conatus.co.uk/assets/uploaded/downloads/policy_and_guidelines_on_supervision.pdf

[9] British Psychological Society. (2010). *Professional supervision: Guidelines for practice for educational psychologists.* Retrieved from http://www.ucl.ac.uk/educational-psychology/resources/DECP%20Supervision%20report%20Nov%202010.pdf

[10] Canadian Psychological Association. (2009). *Ethical guidelines for supervision in psychology: Teaching, research, practice and administration.* Retrieved from http://www.cpa.ca/docs/File/Ethics/EthicalGuidelinesSupervisionPsychologyMar2012.pdf

The *Guidelines for Clinical Supervision in Health Service Psychology*[11] are built on several assumptions, specifically that supervision

- requires formal education and training;
- prioritizes the care of the client/patient and the protection of the public;
- focuses on the acquisition of competence by and the professional development of the supervisee;
- requires supervisor competence in the foundational and functional competency domains being supervised;
- is anchored in the current evidence base related to supervision and the competencies being supervised;
- occurs within a respectful and collaborative supervisory relationship that includes facilitative and evaluative components and is established, maintained, and repaired as necessary;
- entails responsibilities on the part of the supervisor and supervisee;
- intentionally infuses and integrates the dimensions of diversity in all aspects of professional practice;
- is influenced by both professional and personal factors, including values, attitudes, beliefs, and interpersonal biases;
- is conducted in adherence to ethical and legal standards;
- uses a developmental and strength-based approach;
- requires reflective practice and self-assessment by the supervisor and supervisee;
- incorporates bidirectional feedback between the supervisor and supervisee;
- includes evaluation of the acquisition of expected competencies by the supervisee;
- serves a gatekeeping function for the profession; and
- is distinct from consultation, personal psychotherapy, and mentoring.

The importance of supervision can be attested to by the increase in state laws and regulations that certify supervisors and the required multiple supervisory practica and internships that graduate students in all professional programs must complete. Furthermore, research has

---

[11] American Psychological Association. (2014). *Guidelines for clinical supervision in health service psychology.* Retrieved from http://www.apa.org/about/policy/guidelines-supervision.pdf

confirmed[12] the high prevalence of supervisory responsibilities among practitioners—specifically that between 85% and 90% of all therapists eventually become clinical supervisors within the first 15 years of practice.

So now we see the critical importance of good supervision and its high prevalence. We also have guidelines for its competent practice and an impressive list of objectives. But is this enough to become a good supervisor? Not quite. One of the best ways to learn is from highly regarded supervisors—the experts in the field—those who have the procedural knowledge[13] to know what to do, when, and why.

Which leads us to our motivation for creating this series. As we looked around for materials that would help us supervise, teach, and research clinical supervision, we were struck by the lack of a coordinated effort to present the essential models of supervision in both a didactic and experiential form through the lens of expert supervisors. What seemed to be needed was a forum where the experts in the field—those with the knowledge *and* the practice—present the basics of their approaches in a readable, accessible, concise fashion and demonstrate what they do in a real supervisory session. The need, in essence, was for a showcase of best practices.

This series, then, is an attempt to do just that. We considered the major approaches to supervisory practice—those that are based on theoretical orientation and those that are meta-theoretical. We surveyed psychologists, teachers, clinical supervisors, and researchers domestically and internationally working in the area of supervision. We asked them to identify specific models to include and who they would consider to be experts in this area. We also asked this community of colleagues to identify key issues that typically need to be addressed in supervision sessions. Through this consensus building, we came up with a dream team of 11 supervision experts who not only have developed a working model of supervision but also have been in the trenches as clinical supervisors for years.

---

[12] Rønnestad, M. H., Orlinsky, D. E., Parks, B. K., & Davis, J. D. (1997). Supervisors of psychotherapy: Mapping experience level and supervisory confidence. *European Psychologist, 2*, 191–201.

[13] Schön, D. A. (1987). *Educating the reflective practitioner: Toward a new design for teaching and learning in the professions.* San Francisco, CA: Jossey-Bass.

We asked each expert to write a concise book elucidating her or his approach to supervision. This included highlighting the essential dimensions/key principles, methods/techniques, and structure/process involved, the research evidence for the model, and how common supervisory issues are handled. Furthermore, we asked each author to elucidate the supervisory process by devoting a chapter describing a supervisory session in detail, including transcripts of real sessions, so that the readers could see how the model comes to life in the reality of the supervisory encounter.

In addition to these books, each expert filmed an actual supervisory session with a supervisee so that her or his approach could be demonstrated in practice. APA Books has produced these videos as a series and they are available as DVDs (http://www.apa.org/pubs/videos). Each of these books and videos can be used together or independently, as part of the series or alone, for the reader aspiring to learn how to supervise, for supervisors wishing to deepen their knowledge, for trainees wanting to be better supervisees, for teachers of courses on supervision, and for researchers investigating this pedagogical process.

ABOUT THIS BOOK

In this book, *Supervision Essentials for Cognitive–Behavioral Therapy*, Cory F. Newman and Danielle A. Kaplan present a scholarly, yet practical book on cognitive–behavioral therapy (CBT) clinical supervision. In their sophisticated theory-driven approach, these authors use multiple methods of instruction—such as homework, role playing, audiovisual recordings, and Socratic questioning—paralleling the techniques used in doing CBT therapy. But this is not your father's CBT! Drs. Newman and Kaplan challenge our outdated assumptions of CBT principles by focusing, for example, on the importance of the supervisory relationship, with the supervisor serving as a role model of openness. In addition to nitty-gritty how-to's on giving feedback, conducting evaluations, and handling high-risk situations, they also address up-to-date concerns about ethical and multicultural issues. Drs. Newman and Kaplan bring their model alive through real-life supervisory examples designed to demystify the supervisory process. These illustrations describe a succinct and clearly laid out model that supervisors can use to guide the goals and interventions of their supervisory sessions. From setting an agenda and contracting for supervision to assessing outcomes, the supervisor uses CBT techniques to help the supervisee learn how to think like a CBT therapist.

This thoughtful book is an essential read for students and professionals alike; in these pages, there are nuggets of wisdom for novice and experienced supervisors who are committed to evidence-based approaches.

We thank you for your interest and hope the books in this series enhance your work in a stimulating and relevant way.

Hanna Levenson and Arpana G. Inman

Acknowledgments

We would like to express our gratitude to a truly wonderful team of professionals at the American Psychological Association (APA), including Hanna Levenson, who invited us to write this book, and Arpana Inman, Resarani Johnson, and Ed Meidenbauer, who shepherded us through the process of developing the video portion of this project. In particular, Hanna's and Arpana's support has been instrumental in bringing this book to fruition. Additional thanks are due to Tyler Aune, Joanne Revak, and Susan Reynolds for their editorial assistance and to Marla Koenigsknecht for her marketing expertise. We are indebted to Andrew Carlquist, a stellar doctoral student whose participation as the supervisee in the video is a well-earned endorsement of his high level of competency as an early-career cognitive–behavioral therapy (CBT) practitioner. Taking a meaningful look back in time, we were fortunate to have had respective cadres of top-notch clinical supervisors of our own who served as key professional role models. We identify a number of them by name in the Introduction. Here, we collectively wish to pay homage to our esteemed colleagues whose groundbreaking work in the area of evidence-based clinical supervision inspired and informed this book and who are cited liberally throughout the text.

Cory Newman would like to thank Aaron T. Beck and Judith Beck for giving him the opportunity for over two decades to be part of their extramural supervisory team at the Beck Institute for Cognitive Behavior Therapy, which has allowed him to gain valuable cross-cultural experience as he annually supervises their Beck Scholars, chosen from academic institutions throughout North America and around the world. Closer to home, at the University of Pennsylvania, Cory has been privileged to supervise some of the finest clinicians-in-training one will find anywhere and whose enthusiasm, knowledge, and dedication to learning have pushed him to be a better supervisor.

Any skill that Danielle Kaplan has as a CBT supervisor is due in large part to the skilled and dedicated supervision and mentorship she was given during her own training. She is especially grateful to Drs. Donald Baucom and Bernadette Gray-Little, and James O'Keefe, LCPC, JD, for their investment in her development as a clinician and as a professional. Her thanks, too, to Dr. David Greenberg, who gave Danielle her first chance to supervise as a newly minted psychologist.

Danielle was deeply fortunate to have begun her career in New York working for Dr. Robert Leahy at the American Institute for Cognitive Therapy. Dr. Leahy and colleagues at AICT, including Drs. David Fazzari, Lisa Napolitano, Laura Oliff, Jenny Taitz, Dennis Tirch, and Rene Zweig, deepened and broadened her understanding of CBT and the affiliated therapies in ways that continue to inform her own work and supervisory style. She is also grateful to Dr. Leahy for organizing the dinner at which she chanced to sit across from Dr. Cory Newman, without whom her participation in a project like this undoubtedly would have remained an unrealized item on the bucket list. It has been an honor and a pleasure to collaborate with Cory. Danielle's professional life has been greatly enriched by the opportunity to teach and supervise at NYU-Bellevue Hospital Center, academic home to some of the finest psychology externs and interns and psychiatry residents she has known. Deepest thanks to them for continuing to teach and challenge her, and to Drs. Carol Bernstein, Eve Caligor, Ilene Cohen, Alan Elliot, Lucy Hutner, Ze'ev Levin, and Michele Rosenberg for giving her the opportunity to play a role in the design and implementation of CBT training at Bellevue. It is also through her time at Bellevue that Danielle has been given the gift of friendship with Dr. Mark Evces, peer supervisor and business partner extraordinaire. She could not have coauthored this book without the structural, logistical, and unwavering emotional support of her husband, Alan Wolpert. She thanks him for his steady belief in her, for being the mainstay of their family, and for trusting that every wonderful thing they have together would come to be.

Supervision Essentials for

Cognitive–
Behavioral
Therapy

Introduction

Picture the following three scenes, based on true stories from our professional histories:

1. A postdoctoral fellow complains to one of her three supervisors that she is not getting competent supervision. The fellow challenges the supervisor to cite a book he has read on the topic. He goes to his bookshelf and pulls his lone volume on the subject, whereupon the surprised supervisee says, "You're the first supervisor I've ever had who had a book on supervision."

2. The outpatient department of a major hospital-based psychotherapy clinic arranges and holds a clinical supervisors' meeting. The training director explains the importance of formalizing and making such peer supervision meetings routine, at least on a monthly basis. The following month, many of the supervisors fail to attend. The month after that, the meeting is postponed. The supervisors' meetings are never rescheduled.

http://dx.doi.org/10.1037/14950-001
Supervision Essentials for Cognitive–Behavioral Therapy, by C. F. Newman and D. A. Kaplan

3. An experienced cognitive–behavioral therapy (CBT) supervisor receives a voice mail message from a former supervisee who has just gotten his first job as an assistant professor. He explains that one of his new responsibilities is to provide clinical supervision to some of the graduate students in his department. He asks his former mentor, "Could I hire you to give me 'supervision of supervision?' I have never been trained to do supervision, and frankly I'm very anxious."

The delivery of competent clinical supervision is vital to the successful training of therapists and lays the groundwork for the acquisition and maintenance of therapists' high professional standards throughout their careers. Unfortunately, in the history of the field of psychotherapy, the formalized training of new supervisors and the empirical study of supervisory methods and their effectiveness were largely neglected. With regard to the field of CBT in particular, the burgeoning database in support of the efficacy of treatments for a wide range of clinical problems and populations was not matched by a corresponding knowledge base about the key elements of cognitive–behavioral supervision (CBS). It is only in relatively recent times in the field of psychotherapy in general and CBT in particular that the theory, techniques, and empirical bases for competent clinical supervision have begun to be articulated (e.g., Bernard & Goodyear, 2014; Campbell, 2005; Corrie & Lane, 2015; Falender & Shafranske, 2004, 2008; Fleming & Steen, 2012; Hawkins & Shohet, 2012; Kaslow & Bell, 2008; Liese & Beck, 1997; Milne, 2009; Milne, Reiser, Aylott, Dunkerley, Fitzpatrick, & Wharton, 2010; Milne, Sheikh, Pattison, & Wilkinson, 2011; Padesky, 1996; Roth & Pilling, 2008a, 2008b; Scaife, 2001; Sudak et al., 2015; Watkins, 1997, 2011; Watkins & Milne, 2014).

With these publications (and others) as a foundation, the current volume combines the core features of CBT theory and practice with the growing body of empirical findings on competent supervision to present a pragmatically useful primer on how to be an effective CBT supervisor. The tide in the field has turned, and although we are far from having all the answers, we are confident that stories such as the three detailed at the beginning of this introduction will fade into becoming rare exceptions to the rule.

As the field of CBT developed via the empirical testing of treatment packages specifically designed for discrete clinical problems, there was a proliferation of corresponding treatment manuals. In addition to their utility in guiding treatment, such manuals also served to instruct the course of supervision, especially in clinical trials in which supervisors paid particularly close attention to helping therapists adhere to the therapy protocol (see Newman & Beck, 2008). There also has been a movement to identify the commonalities across these separate CBT treatment manuals, selecting key processes that underlie numerous related disorders; this streamlines the task of learning CBT methods that can be widely applied and thus makes the task of conducting therapy and supervision more manageable and less cumbersome (see Barlow et al., 2011; Dobson & Dobson, 2009). Although it does not draw from a unified protocol per se, this handbook adopts the spirit of an approach in which CBS can be described in terms of its general, core principles. As such, it can be used broadly in the oversight of a spectrum of clinical target areas, and supervisees can be guided in their successful application of the most commonly used CBT methods.

THEORETICAL UNDERPINNINGS AND HISTORICAL BACKGROUND

This book owes much of its substance to the field of cognitive therapy as originally developed by Aaron T. Beck (e.g., Beck, 1976; Beck, Rush, Shaw, & Emery, 1979). In the early days of cognitive therapy, the approach was considered distinct from the practice of behavior therapy and viewed as being somewhat different from cognitive–behavioral therapy. Over time, these therapeutic approaches have largely converged (under the broad umbrella that is now CBT), owing in part to their shared theoretical sources and their valuing of measuring and testing the methods, processes, and outcomes of treatment. Therefore, our intent is to represent the overarching principles of CBT and CBS, but our therapeutic language will be most familiar to those who have been trained (and therefore supervised) in a Beckian model.

In two widely cited publications on the topic of CBS (Liese & Beck, 1997; Padesky, 1996), the authors emphasized the strong parallels between the *structure* and *goal-orientation* of CBT sessions and CBS meetings. A key rationale is that a well-organized, well-focused clinical meeting—whether it is between a therapist and client or a supervisor and supervisee—provides fertile ground for learning, the efficient use of time, and the focusing of attention and energy on high-priority topics and goals. The supervision session provides a model for how supervisees can organize their CBT sessions with their clients. When supervisors set an agenda, actively ask open-ended questions, offer and solicit feedback, discuss the use of CBT techniques, focus on the clients' (and sometimes their own and their supervisees') key behaviors and cognitions, engage in experiential methods such as role-playing, and assign and review homework, they are implicitly teaching the supervisees how to get the most out of their work with their clients.

Liese and Beck (1997) and Padesky (1996) also noted that CBT supervisors help their supervisees to think like CBT practitioners, which involves (among other things) conceptualizing clients' problems in terms of their belief systems, identifying the clients' behavioral coping strategies (including strengths and weaknesses therein), and determining which psychological skill sets the clients would need to learn and practice most. Although CBS was not equated with CBT practice, the two had much in common conceptually, with the ultimate goal being to help the supervisees' clients acquire durable cognitive–behavioral self-help skills.

The next advancement in the field of CBS occurred in response to an international trend toward competency-based conceptualizations of clinical supervision (Reiser, 2014). The fact that CBT has emphasized the importance of direct observation and objective standards and measures has given impetus to more writers' attempts to delineate the key components of CBS (e.g., Milne & Dunkerley, 2010; Reiser & Milne, 2012; Roth & Pilling, 2008a). This has gone hand in hand with the growing recognition that learning the skills, knowledge, and professional attitudes to conduct competent supervision needs to be a formalized part of a clinician's training (Falender & Shafranske, 2004, 2007, in press; Kaslow et al., 2004). Within a competencies framework, CBS now shares many characteristics with supervision conducted from other theoretical modalities by virtue of needing to include the essentials of documentation and consultation, ethics mentoring, attention to cross-cultural matters, trainee evaluation and professional gatekeeping, and other pantheoretical elements of training novice therapists. Indeed, this text presents the reader with both the core components of supervising CBT per se and the broader aspects of clinical training and oversight. As such, this text will be of interest to anyone who is active as a clinical supervisor in the mental health care professions, particularly those whose primary area is CBT or who are seeking to familiarize themselves with CBT, and/or who bear the responsibility for training others at the graduate, postdoctoral, or professional level.

As we touch upon in the last chapter on research and future directions, the next evolutionary step (already under way) involves the objective and reliable measurement of explicitly defined supervisory procedures, perhaps in manualized formats, amenable to controlled research (Reiser & Milne, 2012). These procedures center on CBT theory and practice but also are derived from educational principles and research on theories of learning (Reiser, 2014), emphasizing role-play, rehearsal, modeling, and feedback. The chapters ahead are replete with comments on and examples of these methods of supervision.

CBS AS DIFFERENTIATED FROM TREATMENT

Milne (2007) concisely defines supervision (particularly CBS) as "the formal provision, by senior/qualified health practitioners, of an intensive, relationship-based education and training that is case-focused and which supports, directs and guides the work of colleagues" (p. 440). A cognitive–behavioral approach makes a clear delineation between supervision and treatment such that the supervisor does not take on a dual role as a therapist for the supervisee. Having said that, when supervisees encounter difficulties in their work owing to personal experiences such as anxiety, low self-confidence, and life events that lead to distress and distraction, the CBT supervisor will not ignore the matter if it is affecting the supervisee's work. In such instances, the CBT supervisor will compassionately offer general support, collaboratively discuss with the supervisee the degree to which the latter's personal matters are impinging on his or her work with clients, offer constructive feedback to bolster the supervisee's hopefulness, and, if necessary, facilitate the trainee's entering into therapy with a third-party professional.

Pertinent to the matter of the distinction between supervision and treatment in CBT, Newman (1998) summarized similarities and differences across several variables. For example, both the therapeutic relationship (TR) and the supervisory relationship (SR) involve defined roles and a power imbalance that are nonetheless facilitated by an atmosphere of benevolent support, including promoting hopefulness and self-efficacy, within safe, professionally appropriate interpersonal boundaries. In both the TR and the SR, skills are taught, constructive feedback is regularly offered, progress is measured, and there is a spirit of collaboration in which the more "senior" person in the dyad assumes the lion's share of the professional responsibility for how the more "junior" person is faring. On the other hand, the SR does not involve the treatment of the supervisee, the time frame is often tied to an academic calendar (rather than being based on clinical, financial, and/or research parameters), the participants in the SR dyad have a shared responsibility for a third party (the client), and the SR arguably has a more flexible evolutionary path once the supervisee has completed training and is credentialed (e.g., supervisors and supervisees readily become colleagues and can establish a more personal connection in the future, in contrast to therapists and clients, who typically remain in their roles respective to each other long after therapy is completed).

OUR PATH TO CBS EXPERTISE

The following brief sections are personal commentaries from each of the authors, reviewing their respective pathways toward becoming experienced CBT supervisors.

CN: I earned my license as a psychologist in 1989, but prior to that time I had never received formal instruction on how to be a clinical supervisor.

My "how to be a supervisor" road map was composed of my experiences as a trainee who received supervision for the better part of the 1980s, first as a doctoral student at the State University of New York at Stony Brook, then as a clinical psychology intern at the Veterans Administration Medical Center in Palo Alto, California, and finally as a postdoctoral fellow at the Center for Cognitive Therapy at the University of Pennsylvania. I was fortunate to receive supervision from top-notch professionals who were experts in the field as well as genuine supporters of my development as a therapist-in-training. I cannot possibly name all of my former supervisors, but I would like to give special mention to such psychologists as Marvin Goldfried, Tom D'Zurilla, Dan O'Leary, Steve Beach, Tom Burling, James Moses, Bill Faustman, Fred Wright, Art Freeman, Bob Berchick, and Ruth Greenberg. Of course, my chief mentor during my postdoctoral years was a psychiatrist—Aaron T. Beck. Thus, although I never received formal instruction in being a clinical supervisor, I was blessed with many excellent role models from whom I learned by observation. Interestingly, it is highly likely that my mentors never received formal training in supervision themselves.

Within weeks of obtaining my license to practice psychology, I became part of the supervisory team at the Center for Cognitive Therapy and was assigned my first supervisee—a first-year postdoctoral fellow—a position I myself had assumed just 2 years previously. Before long I was assigned additional postdoctoral supervisees as well as third-year and fourth-year psychiatry residents going through CBT rotations at the University of Pennsylvania. Later, I purchased Dryden and Thorne's 1991 handbook *Training and Supervision for Counselling in Action*, which became my primary volume on the topic of clinical supervision for several years. Then, owing to the leadership of Aaron T. Beck, the Center for Cognitive Therapy was constantly running or taking part in clinical trials (on the treatment of panic disorder, substance abuse, depression, bipolar disorder, personality disorders, and other clinical problems), all of which required protocol supervisors. I was assigned the task of supervising five licensed mental health care professionals taking part in the CBT wing of a multisite National Institute on Drug Abuse study on the treatment of cocaine dependence, a trial that ran for several years. As a coauthor of the volume *Cognitive Therapy of Substance Abuse* (Beck, Wright, Newman, & Liese, 1993), I was in a good position to provide the training and supervision that were based on this book.

When Aaron T. Beck and Judith Beck founded the Beck Institute for Cognitive Therapy and Research (now named the Beck Institute for Cognitive Behavior Therapy) in 1994, I was selected to be an adjunct clinical supervisor for an international training program (although I remained as a therapist and supervisor at the Center for Cognitive Therapy, on the faculty at the University of Pennsylvania). Over the years that I have been providing clinical supervision at Penn and via the Beck Institute, I have supervised more than 300 predoctoral externs, postdoctoral fellows, psychiatry residents, protocol cognitive–behavioral therapists in clinical trials, and (via the Beck Institute) extramural fellows and "Beck Scholars," including therapists from five continents. During my sabbatical in the Department of Psychology and Neurosciences at the University of Colorado at Boulder in the fall of 2011 (having obtained my license to practice psychology in Colorado), I provided group supervision to three doctoral students and taught their graduate seminar on learning to become a CBT supervisor.

During my years as a supervisor (still ongoing), I have endeavored to keep up with the literature on supervision, contributing to it myself when possible. As much as I learned from my venerable supervisors back in the 1980s, I must say that I have learned at least as much from my supervisees collectively since that time. I look forward to learning ever more, year after year.

DK: I received my doctorate in clinical psychology from the University of North Carolina at Chapel Hill in 2000. Although our graduate training did not include formal course work in clinical supervision, we were required to take courses in teaching and meet regularly for supervision of our work as undergraduate instructors. Many of the lessons I learned from my program's emphasis on teaching, and especially from Drs. Donald Baucom and Joe Lowman, have been instrumental in laying the foundation for my development as a CBT supervisor.

Upon obtaining my license to practice independently, I immediately began supervising externs and interns at Advocate Illinois Masonic Medical Center, where I had completed my own internship and postdoctoral work. I supervised psychology trainees at all levels while I remained at Illinois Masonic and continued to do so when I moved to New York in 2003 to begin working at the American Institute for Cognitive Therapy (AICT).

It was at AICT, under the direction of Dr. Robert Leahy, that I began to refine my supervisory approach to place more of an emphasis on cognitive–behavioral case formulation and intervention. My time at AICT was invaluable in my development as a supervisor, both because of the opportunities I had to hone and enhance my CBS skills and because of the supervision I received from Dr. Leahy and colleagues at the Institute. During my tenure at AICT, I also had the opportunity to run CBS groups for clinical psychology doctoral students at Yeshiva University's Ferkauf Graduate School of Psychology.

In 2006, I accepted a position at Bellevue Hospital Center as "the cognitive–behavioral therapist" in the outpatient psychiatry clinic. It is a sign of how thoroughly the climate at Bellevue has changed since I began working there that it was then considered notable that I was being hired to work with clients within a cognitive–behavioral framework. My job responsibilities at the time consisted of clinical work, supervising psychology externs and interns, and running the CBT didactics and clinical elective for the psychiatry residency. The residency training component of my position required me to articulate my philosophy of CBS and communicate that philosophy to other supervisors in a way that encouraged and assisted them in promulgating the core competencies of CBT to the resident supervisees.

In 2010, I assumed the directorship of the NYU-Bellevue Predoctoral Psychology Internship. With that position came the responsibility of setting departmentwide policies for clinical supervision. During my time at Bellevue, I have delved deeply into the literature on clinical supervision in general and CBS in particular, including much that has been written by Dr. Newman. I have also had ongoing opportunities to act as both a participant in and a facilitator of discussion groups on supervision within the context of the internship. In this capacity, I have been influenced by many colleagues whose exceptional work has helped me to set a high bar for my own supervisory efforts.

To date, I have been directly responsible for the CBS of more than 150 externs, interns, postdoctoral fellows, psychiatry residents, and licensed professionals and have had ultimate supervisory oversight for the CBT training of more than 100 additional psychology interns and psychiatry residents. Thus, my development as a CBT supervisor also owes a good deal to my many supervisees, who help me to become better at what I do each time I am fortunate enough to share an hour with them.

ROAD MAP TO THE CONTENTS OF THIS BOOK

Our chief goal in writing this book is to give the reader a concise handbook on the key components of effective CBS that can serve as a companion guide for a formal course, as well as a reference book for general use. We draw from the best descriptive literature of years past (e.g., Liese & Beck, 1997; Padesky, 1996), combining it with the ever-growing empirical literature on best practices in clinical supervision (e.g., Bennett-Levy, McManus, Westling, & Fennell, 2009; Milne, Aylott, Fitzpatrick, & Ellis, 2008; Milne, Sheikh, Pattison, & Wilkinson, 2011; Reiser & Milne, 2012). Along the way, we explicate both the clinical components and the administrative aspects of this supervisory model. Our intent is to communicate in a tone that conveys the seriousness of the subject while also modeling the sort of positive, congenial, empathic support that reflects a healthy professional relationship.

The text goes beyond describing how CBT supervisors provide oversight to their trainees in delivering CBT techniques. It makes reference to such important areas as cognitive–behavioral case conceptualization, cross-cultural and ethical competencies in supervision, optimizing both the supervisory relationship and the therapeutic relationship, managing clinical crisis situations via supervision, and professionally administering the documentation and evaluative aspects of supervision. Further, the current volume also touches on the use of group supervision and a model for supervision of supervision (also known as *metasupervision*). With liberal use of case material,[1] this book clearly illustrates the essential knowledge, skills, and attitudinal components of competent CBS. Readers will learn how to use multiple methods of teaching in supervision, including didactic instruction, experiential exercises, audiovisual recordings, and homework assignments. From start to finish, this book demonstrates how to conduct competent CBS with confidence and benevolence, communicating high motivation and enthusiasm for helping trainees develop competency in CBT, and never straying from the primary goal of helping the trainees' clients.

As the title suggests, this book is written from the vantage points of two authors with long professional histories of receiving and providing training in CBT. Nonetheless, the skills, attitudes, and knowledge base that make up competent clinical supervision of any theoretical orientation cover a broad spectrum; consequently this book also describes best practices of supervision that transcend CBT per se. Similarly, it is not our intent to spell out all of the details of CBT-specific methods that supervisors teach, review, model, and support because those methods would go well beyond the scope of a convenient guidebook and are detailed in other CBT texts (e.g., Beck, 2011). It also is not possible for us to give more than a brief explication of the sort of supervision that is provided in clinical trials that use specific CBT manuals for specific clinical problems. As noted, we present CBS consistent with a cross-diagnostic approach (Barlow et al., 2011). Thus, we consider this text to be principle driven more than protocol driven.

Chapter 1 describes essential dimensions and key principles in CBS. These include an explication of the supervisory relationship, the goals that are pursued, the values that are conveyed, the types of CBT methods that supervisees need to learn, the process of contracting for supervision, and the process of evaluating supervisees. Chapter 2, on the topic

---

[1] All case material and supervisory dialogues have been disguised to protect the confidentiality of clients and supervisees, with the exception of Andrew (see Chapter 3), who has given permission to have his session discussed in this book. His clients' identities have been disguised to protect their confidentiality.

of supervisory methods and techniques, takes into account the supervisees' level of development, their individualized training needs, their professional setting, and the differences between individual and group supervision. The importance of clinical documentation in supervision also is noted. The remainder of the chapter focuses on supervision methods such as instruction, modeling, role-playing, and the use of audiovisual recordings. Chapter 3 takes a brief look at what happens in a typical CBS meeting, including a review of the highlights of the companion DVD to this volume,[2] which features one of us (CN) working with an advanced doctoral student in clinical psychology. Chapter 4 provides a look at an array of special issues in supervision, including handling supervisees who pose challenges such as skills deficits or compromised professional functioning that requires remediation. Other special issues include supervisors being responsive to multicultural factors in supervision, promulgating good ethical practices, and sometimes intervening directly with clients in critical situations. Chapter 5 is devoted to the topics of supervisor development, metasupervision, and supervisor self-care, from basic training to continuing education. Chapter 6 provides an overview of the empirical state of the field of CBS, along with a glance at the future of CBS, including early instruction and training across the professional lifespan, global cross-cultural advancements, and the ways that technology continually influences the field. We also suggest sources that allow the reader to pursue a host of relevant matters in greater depth than our convenient guidebook can cover.

Along the way, the reader will notice some overlap of material from one chapter to another. Given that different aspects of CBS are not always readily compartmentalized, such overlap should be viewed as appropriate cross-referencing. In any case, some degree of redundancy is good for long-term retention, as we often see in our work with clients and supervisees alike.

Welcome, and let's continue!

---

[2] *Cognitive–Behavioral Therapy Supervision*, available from APA Books at http://www.apa.org/pubs/videos/4310957.aspx.

1

Essential Dimensions/ Key Principles

THE IMPORTANCE OF THE SUPERVISORY RELATIONSHIP

The centrality of the therapeutic relationship (TR) is widely acknowledged and empirically supported in the field of psychotherapy (see Norcross & Lambert, 2011). However, it may be argued that the salience of the supervisory relationship (SR) is sometimes underestimated (Ladany, 2004). In fact, supervisors must be mindful of creating a safe environment for trainees—safe enough for them to speak freely about the difficulties they may encounter in treating certain clients. Such difficulties may include supervisees' gaps in knowledge about certain clinical problems and/or the proper corresponding interventions or their problematic emotional reactions to clients, such as anger, fear, boredom, and sexual attraction (Ladany, Friedlander, & Nelson, 2005; Ladany, Hill, Corbett, & Nutt, 1996).

http://dx.doi.org/10.1037/14950-002
Supervision Essentials for Cognitive–Behavioral Therapy, by C. F. Newman and D. A. Kaplan

It is incumbent upon the supervisor to contribute to a climate in supervision that encourages trainees to speak candidly and thoughtfully about such matters without the fear of censure, condemnation, or harm to their status in their training/credentialing programs. A key element in formulating an objective evaluation of supervisees' progress in training is listening to or watching audiovisual recordings of therapy sessions conducted by the supervisees. A collaborative, benevolent SR can go a long way toward providing supervisees with both the implicit and the explicit encouragement to submit recordings of their work that may not always show them at their best but may allow the supervisors to give constructive feedback that will assist both the supervisee's and the client's progress. Overall, there is evidence that a positive SR is related to the quality of supervision and to the supervisees' satisfaction with supervision (see Livni, Crowe, & Gonsalvez, 2012).

How can supervisors create such a positive SR? It starts at the first meeting, with the supervisor inviting a discussion about the goals of supervision, and overtly saying things such as,

> It is my responsibility to help you provide your clients with the best care possible while simultaneously promoting your growth as a clinical professional. I intend to give you a lot of constructive feedback along the way so that you know where you stand, so that our work together is a meaningful learning experience for you, and so that you can make adjustments in your approach when necessary. I am very invested in your success in this program, and I am highly motivated to help you achieve your clinical learning goals.

During the course of supervision, it is useful for supervisors to positively reinforce supervisees who take risks in making difficult disclosures about their work with their clients. The following are examples of supervisors' comments that serve this purpose:

- "This new client on your caseload seems to have a history of exhibiting high-risk behaviors, missing sessions, and sometimes making excessive demands on his therapists that require limit setting. Moving forward, we—as a clinical team—are going to give this client the benefit of the doubt in terms of conceptualizing his problems objectively and providing him with interventions that may truly help him. *I will be impressed by anything that you do with this fellow that can help him break old patterns and make progress in treatment.* Similarly, *I will be impressed if you are willing to tell me about the inherent difficulties, including negative cognitive or emotional reactions, you may have at times in working with this client.* If you show that sort of courage it will give me the best chance of working with you to come up with responses that will help both you and your client."

- "When you submit recordings of your sessions with your clients, I will listen to them in their entirety, and I intend to let you know where I think you were on track and also where you may have gone off track, but it will always be with the goal of helping you to help your client. If you can listen to the recording as well and give yourself some corrective feedback, that would be ideal, and I will respect your comments. I will also look at your corresponding clinical note to get a better understanding of your views about the session and what you intended to accomplish. In other words, *I will greatly appreciate you sharing your work samples with me, and I will welcome a constructive dialogue with you about any sticking points you may have in a given session.*"

- (*Upon seeing that the supervisee is somewhat distressed about a particular client*) "I give you credit for facing these problematic issues with this client and for bringing them up in supervision. The easiest thing in the world would be to omit this discussion, put this client last on our agenda, and get a perfunctory signature from me on your note. Instead, *you are highlighting the difficulties you are having with this client, and I commend you for that.* Let's do some problem solving, but first, how are you feeling right now? What do you think about what I just said?"

- (*Chuckling in a good-natured way*) "You don't have to apologize for using the word 'countertransference.' It's not *verboten* in cognitive–behavioral therapy, and in fact I could show you quite a bit of CBT literature that explicitly uses this term, although maybe in different ways than it was originally formulated. I am very open to hearing your views on the matter. What sort of thoughts and feelings did you notice in yourself in working with this client? *I think it's great if you can self-reflect in this manner because it not only will provide us with useful data in supervision but it also will help you to monitor yourself constructively in session so that your behavior remains professional and clinically on target.*"

Whereas CBS is not free of occasional points of disagreement between supervisors and their trainees, the supervisor attempts to be collaborative in discussing and resolving the relevant issues. For example, a supervisor may recommend a particular intervention, whereas the supervisee may favor an alternative approach. Rather than getting into a "competition" about whose intervention is "right," the supervisor can nicely ask the supervisee to offer a rationale for his or her point of view and then to summarize it thoughtfully. Many times, the issue is not a matter of "either/or" as there may be ample reason to try more than one approach such that both the supervisor's and supervisee's hypotheses can be tested appropriately in the next session with the client. When supervisors have reason to believe that their supervisees may be hesitant to offer contrasting points of view, they (the supervisors) can nicely spell out that they welcome supervisees' comments that may not necessarily fall in lockstep with what the supervisors believe. Supervisors can encourage an open consideration of more than one hypothesis because the ultimate goal is to help the clients by following the data rather than by being wedded to one viewpoint or one method.

GOALS

There are two fundamental goals of clinical supervision in general and several subgoals that are pertinent to CBS per se. The primary goal of supervision is to provide clients with care that is properly and competently managed, in which both supervisor and supervisee measure the clients' progress and outcomes (Swift et al., 2015). The supervisor provides the trainee with ongoing feedback and direction so that treatment stays on course and adheres to professional guidelines and mandates, thus ensuring that clients receive at least a normative standard of care. The secondary goal of supervision is to promote the professional development of the supervisees themselves by affording them hands-on clinical experience combined with supportive and corrective instruction. Over time, the supervisors take more of a backseat, asking more of the trainees (e.g., in terms of treatment planning and outcome evaluation), and moving them toward goals such as licensure, independent practice, and specialty areas. When trainees evince significant difficulties in meeting their clinical obligations, perhaps owing to a poor acquisition of basic competencies or perhaps because of compromised functioning, supervisors also have the responsibility of serving as gatekeepers for the profession and for the public. Rather than allowing such substandard trainees to have a perfunctory pass toward graduation, supervisors need to facilitate their trainees' receiving the remediation they need in order to earn the privilege of treating clients. We discuss this important issue again later in the volume.

Facilitating the supervisees' professional development includes teaching them and/or evaluating them on their foundational and functional competencies in conducting psychotherapy in general. These are two of the three categories (along with the developmental level) that make up the Cube Model of psychotherapy competency (Rodolfa et al., 2005), a conceptual framework with which we are most familiar and have found particularly useful. Foundational competencies broadly include the qualities we call "professionalism," such as respecting and understanding the scientific underpinnings of human functioning and mental health care; adhering to ethical standards; being interpersonally effective; valuing self-reflection and self-correction; being sensitive and responsive to cross-cultural issues; diligently keeping clinical records; and knowing how and when to appropriately consult with other professionals on matters pertinent to client care, among other variables.

Complementary to the foundational competencies are the functional competencies that have to do with the specific skills and knowledge base required to provide therapy to clients. In CBT, these include conducting a cognitive–behavioral (and perhaps a formal diagnostic) assessment; collecting clinical data to formulate a cognitive–behavioral case conceptualization and measure clients' progress; devising, implementing, and evaluating the results of specific CBT interventions; and having the requisite knowledge and skills to provide clients with valid, helpful psychoeducational knowledge.

Of course, it is not solely the supervisor's job to introduce the trainees to the foundational and functional competencies of conducting therapy. Extensive course work is part and parcel of trainees' ascension to more advanced levels of professional development and corresponding competence. However, supervisors are important promulgators of this knowledge, by word and by deed. As an example, supervisors can make sure that their therapists-in-training are conversant in the rules and exceptions pertinent to maintaining the confidentiality of client information. Supervisor and trainee can do a role-play in which the supervisor plays the part of the client while the trainee recites his or her monologue about the limits of confidentiality. The supervisor can then offer feedback, perhaps helping the trainee to improve his or her style of delivery of this information so that it has more of a routine and benevolent feel and tone. Throughout the course of the supervisory relationship, the supervisor then "walks the walk" of preserving the client's confidentiality by taking care not to disclose client information in unsecured ways and settings, thus serving as an ethical role model.

The subgoals of CBS (consistent with enhancing functional competencies) include familiarizing the supervisees with the methods of CBT per se, explicating how these methods differ across clinical areas of concern and client populations. At times the clinical supervision is part of a research project in which the supervisors are charged with the task of guiding the therapists through a treatment protocol, making sure that the CBT is delivered with fidelity, and with a minimum of "drift" (see Newman & Beck, 2008; Waller, 2009). At other times the supervision is guided less by circumscribed manuals and more by general CBT principles tailored toward individually based case conceptualizations (e.g., Kuyken, Padesky, & Dudley, 2009) and treatment plans (e.g., Leahy, Holland, & McGinn, 2011). In either instance, effective CBT supervisors help their supervisees learn how to structure therapy sessions for time efficiency and become familiar with delivering a number of specific techniques that are central to CBT overall (e.g., self-monitoring, cognitive restructuring, behavioral activity planning, exposures to avoided experiences, relaxation) as well as methods that are associated with specialty areas within CBT (e.g., mindfulness, guided imagery, values-driven behavioral prescriptions, emotional self-regulation, and self-soothing). In addition, supervisors work with their supervisees to create homework assignments that will help clients practice these methods in their everyday lives.

Thus, there is a pathway of teaching that leads from the supervisor to the clinical trainee and then to the clients themselves. Ultimately, as several studies have suggested, clients who learn and utilize the self-help skills of CBT in a competent way tend to get more out of treatment as a whole (Jarrett, Vittengl, Clark, & Thase, 2011; Strunk, DeRubeis, Chiu, & Alvarez, 2007), just as clients who engage in CBT homework assignments more regularly and with higher quality show better short-term and long-term gains from their participation in CBT (Burns & Spangler, 2000; Kazantzis, Whittington, & Dattilio, 2010; Rees, McEvoy, & Nathan, 2005). Clearly, when CBT supervisors succeed in teaching their clinical trainees to teach their clients—via the use of in-session methods and the use of homework assignments—the all-important goals of promoting better client outcomes and therapist competencies are facilitated.

Another important subgoal can be described as follows: supervisors train their supervisees to learn to think like CBT practitioners, most notably by studying and applying the principles of CBT case conceptualization (Beck, 2011; Eells, 2011; Kuyken et al., 2009; Needleman, 1999; Persons, 2008; Sturmey, 2009; Tarrier, 2006). This involves guiding trainees to become data collectors and hypothesis generators who, with care and interest, seek an increasingly better situational and phenomenological understanding of their clients' lives, taking into account the clients' biohistorical and familial-cultural contexts. It also involves thinking across disciplines, such as when a medical problem may be playing a role in the client's difficulties. Here, supervisees need to give consideration to the possibility that they may need to refer their clients for a medical examination (e.g., an endocrinology work-up), neuropsychological testing, or other forms of assessment pertinent to their health and overall functioning that may go beyond the scope of standard CBT.

The following sample dialogue between a supervisor and clinical trainee illustrates the process of teaching the trainee to think and conceptualize in CBT terms. The trainee at first states that the client's behavior "doesn't make sense," whereupon the supervisor encourages the trainee to generate hypotheses that may help explain the client's in-session reactions and shed light on how to intervene in an accurately empathic way.

Trainee: My client spends a lot of time in session bitterly complaining about not being appreciated, either in her personal life or at work. She gives me example after example about her friends taking her for granted and not giving back what she gives them. Almost every session she tells me that nobody gives her credit for her contributions at work and that she is constantly being overlooked despite her hard work. But here's a funny thing. A pattern has developed in our therapeutic relationship where I give her positive feedback—such as telling her that I admire her sense of responsibility at work or that I think she has been very resilient in the face of disappointments—and then she doesn't acknowledge what I've said at all. She changes the subject or just keeps complaining. She comes across as craving positive acknowledgment in her life, but when I try to give that to her, she seems to ignore it. It makes no sense.

Supervisor: Well, it's certainly a paradox. She purports to want something from people, then you give it to her, and she appears not to notice it. It's incongruous. But maybe in a way it "makes sense" in her world. Can you try to come up with a hypothesis or two that might explain this pattern? Mind you, I'm not saying that you have to know for sure. We don't have enough clinical data for that sort of accuracy or certainty yet. But this is a good opportunity for you to look for the "logic in the illogic." How might this all make sense?

Trainee: Well, the thought crossed my mind earlier that maybe she doesn't perceive the positive feedback for some reason. I was thinking that maybe she has some sort of mental filter that for some reason does not allow her to really hear or incorporate people's positive comments toward her. That might account for her really believing that nobody appreciates her and for her not seeming to notice the support I'm giving her.

Supervisor: What sort of "filter" or schema might we be talking about here?

Trainee: I guess this could be an example of an "unlovability" or "social exclusion" schema. I actually thought of that, but there's another problem. I tried addressing this issue directly with her. I made a process comment, which is something you and I have practiced through role-playing in supervision. I told her that I noticed that every time I felt something genuinely positive about her to the extent that I came out and told her directly, she changed the subject and never engaged with me. And do you know what she did? She changed the subject again! I couldn't even make a process comment with her. So I don't think she couldn't perceive the positive regard I was giving her. It seemed like a deliberate avoidance on her part. That's why I couldn't make sense of it.

Supervisor: Nice going with the process comment! That was one of the things I was going to suggest, but you beat me to it. Good work. But since she confounded your attempt to address the issue, we may have to come up with additional hypotheses. What else could be going on here?

Trainee: Maybe she mistrusts the positive comments. Maybe she thinks it's all insincere and that it's a way for people to manipulate her. But she hasn't said anything like that before, so I think this "mistrust" schema hypothesis could be a bit of a stretch. It's also possible that we're talking about a "vulnerability to harm" schema in that if she allows herself to believe that someone has positive regard for her she might become too attached, and she might be afraid of that. I'm just concerned that I'm getting a little too wild with my hypotheses here.

Supervisor: Well, if you can perceive my positive feedback and can allow yourself to trust it (*chuckles*), I have a lot of positive reactions to what you're saying. First of all, that's excellent brainstorming you're doing. Rather than just feeling helpless in the face of client reactions that at first glance seem not to make sense, you are indeed trying to understand the "logic in the illogic," and you are giving consideration to several hypotheses. Second, I have to give you extra credit for recognizing that there is a potential hazard in getting carried away with our armchair hypothesizing. We need to balance the benefits of brainstorming with the potential drawbacks of straying too far from the data. So what can we do about that? How can we stay closer to the data while still keeping an open mind?

Trainee: I can go back and look at previous documentation on the case. I have an intake report from 3 months ago to which I can refer. I also have a copy of a summary submitted by her previous therapist from a few years ago and my own clinical notes from earlier in our work together. Maybe there are clues there that might lend support—or not—to some of the hypotheses about various schemas that we're coming up with.

Supervisor: Bingo! Look at the client's history. Part of this information can be found in the clinical documentation. Another part could be . . .

Trainee: . . . talking directly with the client about her experiences in the past when she was neglected, let down, or otherwise felt unappreciated. Or maybe when she felt manipulated by someone's sweet-talking her. Or maybe when she believed she got too close to someone and then couldn't bear it when she lost them. Or whatever. It's about looking at the history and talking directly to the client about the issues.

Supervisor: Absolutely. You can tell her that you would greatly value her input about her personal history and how it affects the present and that you would welcome her viewpoints about your clinical hypotheses. That's another great way to stay close to the data. I know that you said that you already tried to make a process comment with her to no avail, but maybe it will take several times and several variations to reach her with your sincere comments. How about if we try to role-play some ways that you could try to make more of such process comments to her? Who do you want to be first: the client or the therapist?

In the previous dialogue, the CBT supervisor encourages the trainee to brainstorm schema-focused conceptual hypotheses while agreeing that it is important to stay close to the facts of the case as known and as could be gained through further inquiry. Note that the supervisor offers a good deal of constructive, supportive feedback.

Another subgoal of supervision is helping trainees properly manage and administrate the termination or transfer of their work with clients.

The importance of a client's ending treatment on a constructive, positive note is analogous to the importance of someone's successfully graduating from school with confidence, hope, and credentials. Similarly, the necessity of smoothly transferring a graduating trainee's clients to a new therapist who can seamlessly continue to provide proper treatment is as relevant as a hospital patient's receiving consistent care from one shift of nurses to the next. Supervisors help orchestrate the manner in which the trainees accomplish the goal of a healthy termination or transfer first by keeping track of the status of each client (including client absences from treatment) and second by being aware of the supervisees' target dates for finishing their current period of training. The proper handling of therapy terminations and transfers has major clinical and ethical implications (Davis, 2008), so it is incumbent upon supervisors to make sure that no client "falls through the cracks" in the system.

Supervisors serve as procedural advisors to their supervisees about how to prepare clients for the end of their work together, both from a practical, administrative standpoint and from a clinical standpoint (e.g., sensitively dealing with clients who feel a profound sense of anticipatory loss, and/or anxiety, and/or anger). They also serve as ethical mentors, helping supervisees understand how to steer clear of the two dysfunctional extremes of termination—abrupt abandonment of the client on the one extreme and seeing clients for extended periods of time with no evidence of therapeutic benefit (or without attempting any adaptations to the treatment plan) at the other extreme. In sum, supervisors play a vital role in helping supervisees learn to create a positive resolution to their work with their clients.

Supervisors, by their words and deeds, communicate a set of values to their trainees (see Corrie & Lane, 2015; Falender & Shafranske, 2004), which is an oft-overlooked subgoal of supervision. Although many of these values are subsumed under the ethical principles that are formally codified and guide the field of mental health care, there are parallel values that are not often explicitly articulated but that warrant mention in their own right. The list that follows is neither exhaustive nor universal, and its contents may be modifiable depending on cultural context. However, it is useful to spell out the sorts of attitudes and beliefs that many CBT supervisors try to inculcate in their trainees through modeling. The following items are adapted from Newman (2012):

- Time is precious. Therefore competent therapists strive to be time-effective both in session and over a course of treatment.
- Learning CBT well requires repetitions. If we apply the methods of CBT to ourselves routinely, thus providing ourselves with more practice, it will benefit our professional development as well as our personal well-being.
- Stay close to the twin priorities of teaching clients solid, durable self-help skills and boosting their morale and sense of hope.
- Hypothesis generation and testing are far preferable to self-assured dogmatism.
- Embrace the role of being an ever-learning student for your entire career.
- To gain the trust and collaboration of a client is a privilege not a right.
- To truly understand and empathize with clients, endeavor to see the world through their eyes.
- Words matter. They can hurt, and they can heal. Communicate with kindness and clarity.

Other writers have included such values as the importance of tolerating (indeed, embracing) ambiguity, rather than being disconcerted when real-life clinical practice does not imitate the textbooks, and looking at high affect in clients and oneself not as a distraction but as an opportunity for better understanding (see Friedberg, Gorman, & Beidel, 2009; Safran & Muran, 2001). Yes, supervisees need to have respect for the fundamentals of CBT practice, but they can benefit from discovering the art of "flexibility within fidelity" (Kendall, Gosch, Furr, & Sood, 2008; Newman, 2015).

TEACHING CBT METHODS

Discussing the care of ongoing clients provides fertile ground for the explication of any number of CBT practice methods. Although there are many excellent books on the topic of learning and utilizing CBT techniques that can be assigned to supervisees for homework (e.g., Beck, 2011;

Kuyken et al., 2009; Leahy, 2003; Ledley, Marx, & Heimberg, 2010; Newman, 2012; O'Donohue & Fisher, 2009), the supervisor is in an ideal position to assist the supervisee in learning, applying, and practicing CBT techniques. In other words, supervisors help instruct supervisees not only about what to do but also how to do it (Bennett-Levy, 2006; Friedberg et al., 2009), thus turning their supervisees' raw skills into refined skills (Newman, 2010).

Supervisors also play an important role in helping supervisees deal with typical obstacles in implementing techniques, such as how to assign homework and ask for feedback and yet end sessions on time, how to balance a directive approach with guided discovery, and how to respond when clients habitually say, "yes, but. . . ." As an illustration, the following dialogue shows a supervisor providing a recommendation about how the supervisee can improve the client's use of thought records.

Supervisor: I'm glad you made copies of your client's thought records so we could take a closer look at them. I notice that most of the client's comments under the "automatic thoughts" column are in the form of questions. For example, she writes, "Why is this happening to me?" and "What if I never figure out how to cope with my anxiety?"

Trainee: I noticed that, too. It makes it a little tricky to come up with rational responses.

Supervisor: Here's a suggestion. Ask the client to answer her own questions. For example, what are her hypotheses about "why these things always happen" to her and about what is going to happen in the future in terms of her skills in coping with anxiety? We want to draw out her implicit answers to her questions because those are actually her automatic thoughts.

Trainee: My guess is that if we try to hypothesize answers to her questions, we'll find a lot of hopeless and self-reproachful thoughts, such as, "I'm so weak and damaged I'll never get better."

Supervisor: Good guess! And you can see how important it would be to start working on coming up with alternative responses to those sorts of thoughts.

Trainee: I think we'll get a lot more mileage out of identifying automatic thoughts this way. Next session, if my client asks a rhetorical question that sounds distressed, I'm going to nicely ask her to try to answer her own question and create her own hypotheses, and we'll take it from there.

Supervisor: While we're talking about thought records, let me mention another tip. Your client tends to think in "all or none" terms, and therefore it would be great practice for her to generate some rational responses even if she does not believe in them 100%. Can you think of a rationale you can give her for this approach?

Trainee: I guess I could tell her that it's good practice to consider viewpoints other than her more customary depressive and anxious thoughts, even if she doesn't buy into them all the way.

Supervisor: Exactly right. Rational responding doesn't require clients to completely relinquish what they believe in favor of completely adopting new ideas. This is CBT, not reprogramming! Good CBT just asks people to stretch and flex their thinking—like "cognitive yoga"—to consider new ideas that might work better for their mood and functioning.

Trainee: And that means being able to brainstorm, right?

Supervisor: Right. It's about getting them out of their cognitive habits—their tunnel vision. If your client can generate new ways of thinking, it will be helpful, even if she only believes the rational responses at a low level at first, such as 20%.

Trainee: I can see how that will give her evidence against her idea that you either believe something or not, with nothing in between. This strategy will encourage her to write down some rational responses that she might have previously rejected because she didn't totally buy them.

Supervision: So, in the next session, ask the client to answer her own rhetorical questions to get at the actual automatic thoughts that are statements, and then ask her to brainstorm some rational responses along with listing the respective percentages that she believes them.

The didactic part of being a clinical supervisor entails not only teaching supervisees about how to implement the core methods of CBT but also giving general instructions that will help the supervisees to stay on task and be effective clinicians in general. The following is a nonexhaustive sample list of 10 of such nuggets that good CBT supervisors may impart to their trainees. Note that these comments may pertain to CBT in particular but may just as easily reflect best practices regardless of theoretical model.

1. "The sessions you conduct will automatically be better organized and more instructive to the clients if you have good 'bookends.' In other words, start and end your sessions in a strong way, which means that you orient your client to be ready to get to work at the top of the hour, and you summarize the work you have done at the end of the hour so as to maximize what the client takes from the session. For example, if we take a lesson from the Cognitive Therapy Rating Scale (Young & Beck, 1980), a strong opening means that you check on the client's mood, set an agenda, and inquire about the previous homework assignment. A strong finish means that you provide the client with a summary statement about the session, ask the client for feedback about the session, and collaboratively devise a new or continued homework assignment. If you can get into the positive habit of providing these sturdy bookends to your sessions, it will make the entire therapy session more time-effective, relevant, and memorable. Similarly, it is helpful to have strong bookends for the entire course of therapy. A strong first session introduces clients to the treatment model and illustrates how it is relevant to their concerns, shows them that you are a credible professional who is well-equipped and motivated to help them, boosts their sense of hope, and immediately presents them with some early skills and homework. A strong concluding session summarizes your work together, reinforces a maintenance plan, and promotes a sense of camaraderie in which you and your clients contemplate your positive connection and a job well done."

2. "As you begin to use your CBT conceptualization and intervention methods, you may find that it's difficult to relax and just be yourself. After all, when you're working so hard on method it's not so easy to

focus on manner. But don't worry because the more you practice, the more you will find that you can weave your best personal qualities into the interventions so that the therapeutic relationship is strong and you can feel more natural in doing your work. Don't feel that you have to subjugate your personality to the model. I'm confident that you will find that you can succeed in combining best practices in CBT with the best of your personal style. The result will be that you will enjoy the work more, and your clients will benefit greatly."

3. "Clients vary in how much they are willing to engage in the homework assignments. When they are not so keen to do the homework, don't give up. In other words, don't let the clients' lack of positive response extinguish your appropriate homework-giving behavior! Instead, hypothesize what might be getting in the way. Ask the client for feedback. Consider the possibility that the assignment needs to be more specific to the needs of a particular client or that you can do more to explain the assignment and demonstrate how it's done. Maybe the client harbors some negative beliefs about homework, owing to such factors as low confidence, mistrust, sensitivity to interpersonal control, or other issues. Maybe clients will be more willing to take charge and give themselves an assignment if you give them the chance to do so. In other words, make the process more collaborative. In any event, nicely and consistently show clients that you want to give them every opportunity to succeed in therapy, and doing homework has been shown to be one of the key ingredients in what makes CBT work. You can tell clients that they can still benefit from CBT even if they don't do the homework, but add that you want to increase their chances even more, and that's why you're willing to keep giving assignments, in the hope that they will come around at some point and thus will benefit more. Don't let it be a power struggle. Homework should be more of a benevolent offering."

4. "When you give your clients a homework assignment, feel free to announce to them that you are giving yourself a corresponding homework assignment. For example, your homework could be reading the remainder of their journal writings that you didn't have time to discuss

in the session, or it could be reading part of the same self-help book that you are asking them to read, or taking their advice to read or view something that will teach you something about their culture, or any other appropriate assignment that shows that you are willing to practice what you preach. Obviously you don't have to do this every session, and with every client because that might be unwieldy. Nonetheless, for those times when you overtly give yourself an assignment, it can be a nice finishing touch to a session, like a demonstration of solidarity with the client."

5. "We have to remember that we as clinicians are not the final judges about what makes sense and what doesn't make sense in the lives of our clients. If we endeavor to 'walk a mile in their shoes,' then there will be times when we can understand why clients do or believe things that look 'irrational' to the naked eye. To be accurately empathic, and to maximize collaboration, we as clinicians need to look for the 'function in the dysfunction and the logic in the illogic.' By doing so, clients will be more apt to believe we 'get it,' and they may feel more accepted and may become willing to consider making changes."

6. "I know you're trying to be vigilant about the client's negative thoughts and trying to effect change—and I applaud the fact that you are working so hard—but it may be better if you reduce the frequency and the vehemence of your attempts to get the client to engage in rational responding. First of all, it's more efficient and it creates a better flow of therapeutic dialogue if you listen and collect examples of the client's thinking style. Second, by having patience and occasionally summarizing, not only will you be more relaxed but there also will be less risk that the clients will feel like you're micromanaging their thoughts. Third, bear in mind that not all of your interventions will 'take' on the spot. Sometimes the best you can do is to 'plant seeds'—you know, by providing a few key reframes of what the clients are thinking— and then see if some of those seeds sprout over the coming weeks. I used to be overzealous with some clients early in my career, totally with good intentions, just like you. It was as if I had the dysfunctional belief, 'Nobody leaves this office until their cognitions are changed!' We don't have to have that belief."

7. "Take the time to learn the finer details of your clients' lives. Learn the names of the significant people in their lives and their most important dates on the calendar, such as birthdays and happy and sad anniversaries. Remember where they went to school, what they do for a living, where they have lived, and other details that will help you to know them as individuals. If you invest the time to gather these sorts of facts, you will be able to allude to them from time to time in the course of your therapeutic dialogue, and this will solidify the therapeutic relationship. Your clients will see that you know them as individuals and not just as a name on your schedule."

8. "Go the extra mile to write good clinical notes for each therapy session, and please do this promptly while things are still fresh in your mind. Then, before the next session, review the notes you wrote from the previous session so that you are optimally oriented to the issues on which you and your client are working. This will help you feel better prepared and more organized, and it will greatly help you to set a relevant agenda. In addition, you will be serving as a role model for the client. After all, if you can remember the details of a given client's therapy session from last week, the client likely will see the merits in remembering what happened in his or her own previous sessions."

9. "Good therapy is a mutual education process. You are the expert in CBT, but your clients are the experts on what it feels like to be them. Exchange information. Sometimes clients will be more willing to accept your assessment comments and proposed interventions if you have been willing to let them educate you first. By the way, this is not only a beneficial stance to take in treating a given client, but it is also true with regard to your professional development. Clients have a lot to teach us about all sorts of things. For example, they may have gone through life-cycle events you have not yet reached but that you could benefit from understanding a bit better. Similarly, your clients can teach you a great deal about their culture. Be receptive to being a student, even with your clients."

10. "If you have diligently, earnestly applied a CBT case conceptualization and its corresponding treatment approach to a given client, but

the client is not improving, don't despair and don't assume that you are being ineffective or that your client is just being 'difficult.' Consider the possibility that the case may be more complex than you first thought. Maybe the diagnosis needs to be revisited. Maybe there is something going on in the client's personal life outside the clinic that is interfering with treatment. Maybe there is a medical condition that needs to be considered. In other words, ask yourself, 'What data are we missing? Is there important clinical information that the client has not yet disclosed for some reason?' Please bear in mind how difficult it must be to reveal things such as suicidal feelings, or to talk about a trauma history, or to come out as a sexual minority, or to disclose an addiction. Then think about how you can create an environment in which it will be safe enough for clients to explore such weighty subjects if they haven't done so thus far. But don't give up on clients or yourself just because progress is slow to occur."

Another important skill that the CBT supervisor would do well to assess is the supervisee's facility in answering a new client's questions about CBT. This is an anticipated interaction that can be role-played in supervision so that the supervisor can gauge how clearly the supervisee can explain the cognitive–behavioral model of treatment. Related to this psychoeducational skill is the supervisee's ability to address the client's concerns or questions about the official diagnosis (if one has been proffered).

As noted, supervisors offer their supervisees didactic information about CBT and opportunities to practice the skills that emanate from such information. Therapists do the same for their clients. In terms of supplemental didactics, supervisors and their supervisees can discuss which CBT self-help books (or other relevant psychological literature for the informed layperson) can be recommended to which clients. Well-known CBT books such as *Mind Over Mood* (Greenberger & Padesky, 2015) and *The Feeling Good Handbook* (Burns, 1999) are widely read by clients as "take-home guides" that accompany their treatment, and many CBT therapists-in-training are familiar with these seminal manuals. However, there are any number of other high-quality CBT-related books on a wide range of topics (e.g., on overcoming problems associated with the full range of diagnostic areas, utilizing mindfulness, coping with life stressors, helping loved ones) that may be assigned to clients, and supervisors are in a good position to endorse their use. In addition, there are important texts that are not specific to CBT per se that are nonetheless potentially helpful to clients, including such classics as Victor Frankl's (1959) *Man's Search for Meaning* and Kay Redfield Jamison's (1995) *An Unquiet Mind*. Supervisors who are personally familiar with such writings may instruct their supervisees to read one or more of these publications, both for general professional growth and to be better informed about their potential usefulness as homework assignments for their clients. An important point about assigning readings is that it is advisable for the therapists and/or their supervisors to have first-hand familiarity with the material before asking clients to read it.

There are other characteristics of effectiveness as a therapist that are somewhat difficult to quantify but that we hypothesize may enhance the delivery and impact of therapy. Although not routinely mentioned in therapy manuals, these characteristics are ripe for discussion and modeling in supervision. Such qualities have been described by some authors as "meta-competencies" (see Corrie & Lane, 2015; Newman, 2012; Roth & Pilling, 2007), and they include (but are not limited to): (a) clarity of communication style; (b) good sense of timing in delivering interventions (e.g., being fully prepared to discuss a highly sensitive and heretofore sidestepped topic the moment the client alludes to it); (c) excellent memory for the details of clients' lives, their case conceptualizations, and the contents of previous sessions; (d) a wide range of verbal repertoire, tone of voice, and empathic nonverbals; (e) appropriate use of humor (in which the client and therapist laugh together, lighten the mood, and bond a bit more); (f) facility in being well organized so that clients are tended to (and corresponding documentation and consultation managed) in a thorough and prompt manner; and (g) the resiliency to impart an air of hopefulness, encouragement, and steadfast commitment to help, even when clients are entrenched in hopelessness and helplessness. These are the sorts of qualities that help make therapy more memorable and inspirational for clients, thus facilitating the clients' retention and maintenance of important therapeutic principles and their motivation to participate more fully in the process of treatment. Such meta-competencies begin with the supervisor.

SETTING EXPECTATIONS FOR SUPERVISION

Supervisees benefit from learning early on what is expected of them and what they can expect from their supervisors. From a practical standpoint, supervisees should be given at least a rough estimate of the number of clients they will need to treat, over what time frame, in what format of supervision (e.g., individual and/or group), with how many supervisors, and using which methods of documentation (e.g., written vs. electronic), among other topics. Supervisors have a choice about how collaborative they wish to be in establishing expectations about supervision. In some settings, the institutional rules and culture may require supervisors to impose set parameters of supervision. If the environment is more flexible, supervisors can initiate a collaborative conversation with supervisees about the sorts of expectations that may be most appropriate. This discussion may be in the form of a "needs assessment" (Corrie & Lane, 2015; Milne, 2009), in which supervisors ask the supervisees directly about their perceived strengths and weaknesses, their previous training experiences, their sense of self-efficacy in and familiarity with certain types of clients and clinical problems, and their opinions about what they need to work on the most to become more competent overall. As such, a needs assessment may allow for supervisors to tailor a course of clinical training to the specific needs of each supervisee. At the same time, the supervisees will be aware of what they have to work on to grow as professionals. This sort of clarity is good for the entire supervision enterprise.

Likewise, supervisees benefit from knowing what they can expect from their supervisors: for example, how often will they meet (once per week?) and how long will each meeting last (a "50-minute hour?"). If the supervisor is unavailable for any reason, will he or she provide a backup or on-call supervisor for the trainee? Under what conditions should the trainee consult with the supervisor between formal, scheduled supervision sessions? Should such extrasupervisory contacts occur only in a clinically critical situation, or are routine questions okay? Under what conditions will the supervisor directly meet with the supervisee's client(s)? For example, will the supervisor meet with the supervisee's client(s) as a matter of routine, or will this happen only in crisis situations? How often will the supervisor provide formal, summative feedback? Indeed, setting expectations in supervision goes both ways.

These expectations can be spelled out in the form of a supervisory contract. Exhibit 1.1 demonstrates a section of a sample contract, which includes the supervisee's required activities, the types of competencies the supervisee is aiming to acquire, and the responsibilities of the supervisor. As such, it is a document that is congruent with a collaborative professional relationship (Thomas, 2007).

EVALUATION OF THE SUPERVISEE

Supervisors necessarily keep track of the progress of the clients being seen in treatment by their supervisees because their well-being is of paramount importance. At the same time, supervisors actively keep tabs on the progress of their supervisees in learning the foundational and functional competencies of delivering CBT. Supervisors evaluate their supervisees regularly during the course of their work together by giving routine feedback, also known as *formative* evaluation. This can be done at every supervisory session by commenting on various aspects of the trainees' management of their cases, including their handling of the therapeutic relationship; their case conceptualizations; treatment plans; level of proficiency in the use of specific techniques and homework assignments; clarity, accuracy, and thoroughness of their session notes; degree of professionalism in their behaviors and attitudes; demonstrations of thoughtful self-reflection; and responsiveness to supervisory feedback itself. This is quite a substantial list of factors about which to be aware and on which to comment. Although it would be easy to give short shrift to this part of the supervisor's job, perhaps to focus solely on how the clients are progressing in treatment, there is evidence that the quality of supervision is significantly improved when supervisors make it a point to provide their

Exhibit 1.1

Sample "Supervisory Contract" Document Items

I agree to . . .

1. Maintain a caseload of "n" clients for a period of approximately 12 months.
2. Write all therapy notes and reports promptly, and maintain them in an organized fashion in the client's chart so they may be cosigned by the supervisor.
3. Protect my clients' confidential information by keeping the charts in a secure place, using disguised information in case conferences, refraining from discussing cases outside of the training sessions, and using password protection or encryption when sending digital transmissions of client data (e.g., session recordings).

I will learn to . . .

1. Create written cognitive–behavioral conceptualizations for each case.
2. Structure sessions for good time management and good organization of material.
3. Utilize a range of cognitive–behavioral interventions and homework assignments.
4. Foster and maintain healthy, appropriate therapeutic relationships with clients.
5. Learn to use self-reflection to assist my work.

I can expect that my supervisor will . . .

1. Give me constructive feedback in supervision.
2. Listen to at least four full-length recordings of my therapy sessions over the course of 12 months and provide me with ratings on the Cognitive Therapy Rating Scale (CTRS).
3. Provide me with four formal summaries of my progress as a cognitive–behavioral therapist over the course of 12 months.
4. Take professional, ethical, and legal responsibility for the welfare of the clients.

trainees with ongoing feedback both positive and reflective of areas for improvement (Milne, 2009; Milne, Sheikh, et al., 2011).

It is particularly useful if supervisors take the time and make the effort to observe actual work samples, such as audiovisual recordings of their trainees' session(s) with clients. Although this activity is often time intensive, it is the best way to assess the quality of the supervisees' actual in-session work. When time is limited, the supervisor may opt to watch only a segment of a supervisee's session, perhaps to give feedback or suggestions on a discrete issue as it occurred. On the other hand, if the supervisor intends to do a formal rating of the supervisee's adherence to the CBT model and/or competence in delivering the treatment, it is necessary to observe the entire session. As noted, competent supervisors must create an atmosphere of support so that the supervisees will be more likely to submit their recordings with a minimum of trepidation and with the positive expectation that they will receive useful, constructive guidance. When the supervisees make the extra effort to create these recordings, the supervisors should review them as soon as possible both as a sign of respect for the work of the supervisee (and thus to positively reinforce it) and to provide timely clinical feedback.

In addition to providing routine, ongoing feedback, supervisors also periodically provide their supervisees with summative evaluations, which become a formal part of the supervisees' record in their training program. Official summative evaluations of trainees that are subpar may potentially have a negative impact on the trainee's future in the field and thus need to be written in such a way that the critique is constructive and spells out the supervisee's ongoing training needs in as hopeful and respectful a way as possible.

If routine feedback has been given properly, such that supervisees know where they stand at any given time, the summative evaluations will be a natural extension of the process, and the supervisees are likely to perceive congruence and fairness in their evaluations. Summative evaluations should not surprise or shock supervisees with unexpected critiques that have not been discussed previously (see Davis, 2008). Instead, corrective feedback should be given in such a way that the supervisees have ample opportunity to work on shoring up their weaknesses. Summative evaluations ought to be based on a number of concrete factors, such as the timeliness and contents of the supervisees' clinical notes, the supervisees' punctuality and attendance in supervision and meeting with their clients, their case write-ups (e.g., formal case conceptualizations), their scores on measures of their in-session adherence to and competence in delivering CBT (e.g., on the Cognitive Therapy Rating Scale, Young & Beck, 1980; Blackburn et al., 2001), and the objectively measured progress of the clients (e.g., reduction in suicidal ideation and gestures, stable improvements on self-report inventories, corroborating indicators of improvement, such as reports from clients' family members and/or consulting professionals on the same case). Using a combination of such measures lends credibility to the supervisors' feedback, gives the supervisees a more accurate and objective way to assess their own progress in training, and overtly indicates areas in which the supervisees can strive to improve their work.

Whether the supervisors are providing formative or summative evaluations, it is important that they do not fall prey to what has been dubbed in the literature as "the tyranny of niceness" (Fleming, Gone, Diver, & Fowler, 2007), whereby supervisors fear being anything other than supportive of their supervisees and thus avoid giving them the sort of direct, constructively critical feedback that may be essential to their professional development. We agree that it is vitally important for the supervisors to promote a positive, hopeful atmosphere in supervision in which the trainee can flourish, but we also believe that a measure of supervisors' competence is their ability to be supportive of and invested in the supervisees' progress as clinicians even as they are pointing out areas that need further work. In doing so, supervisors serve as role models for their supervisees, who themselves undoubtedly will need to balance genuine support with corrective feedback in their work with clients. Giving supervisees constructive feedback also helps ensure the proper treatment of the clients, which is the top priority.

In contrast to the tyranny-of-niceness phenomenon is the problem of supervisors who take a "no news is good news" approach in providing feedback. Such an approach can give supervisees the mistaken impression that they are underperforming, when in fact the supervisor is silently thinking that much of the work is "obviously" going well. A lack of feedback is often cited by therapists-in-training as an example of a poor supervisory experience (Phelps, 2011). Indeed, the supervisor's failure to provide supervisees with adequate performance evaluations is a surprisingly frequent ethical violation (see Ladany, Lehrman-Waterman, Molinaro, & Wolgast, 1999).

It can also be useful to give supervisees the opportunity to evaluate their supervisors in return given that supervisors potentially have much to learn about how their trainees are perceiving and receiving their work in supervision. Such feedback can help supervisors to make adjustments in their approaches and help administrators who are in charge of an organization's supervision infrastructure, policies, and assignments to address any problems in their program of supervision. However, we must remember that supervisees are in a vulnerable position when it comes to giving potentially critical feedback to their supervisors because they may fear retaliation, with implications for their standing in a training program. Thus, it is best if such feedback can be given anonymously. Clearly, this has to be handled carefully as many training programs are sufficiently small that it would be fairly easy to surmise which supervisee wrote what about whom. A less formal method of eliciting feedback from supervisees can take place as a routine occurrence in each supervision session, simply as a way to "check in" and see how the meeting went that day. This procedure can be viewed as part of the structure of a supervision session, analogous to the therapist's asking for feedback from clients in each therapy session. The supervisor's friendly and inviting demeanor can reassure the trainee that the purpose of such feedback is to improve the supervisory experience. A running theme throughout this text is that supervisors have authority and power, but they must use this authority and power wisely and benevolently. Nowhere is this more evident and important than in the area of providing and receiving evaluative feedback.

2

Supervisory Methods/Techniques

This chapter takes a look at some of the methods that are used in cognitive–behavioral supervision (CBS) to help supervisees learn to become competent (and ultimately proficient) in cognitive–behavioral therapy (CBT) and to be vigilant in tracking and documenting what transpires in their sessions with clients. First, we consider how the supervisee's level of professional development and the clinical setting in which the supervisee trains affect the supervisor's expectations.

http://dx.doi.org/10.1037/14950-003
Supervision Essentials for Cognitive–Behavioral Therapy, by C. F. Newman and D. A. Kaplan
Copyright © 2016 by the American Psychological Association. All rights reserved.

EXPECTATIONS DEPENDING UPON THE SUPERVISEE'S DEVELOPMENT AND THE CLINICAL SETTING

Therapists who are about to commence receiving clinical supervision do so from a wide range of developmental starting points. For example, a supervisee may be one of the following:

- A new graduate student who is about to treat clients for the first time.
- An advanced graduate student who has been accepted to a competitive practicum.
- A predoctoral intern who now is responsible for his/her largest caseload to date.
- A postdoctoral fellow who is seeing clients to accumulate hours for licensure.
- A newly licensed mental health professional who is legally and professionally permitted to treat clients in independent practice but who nonetheless seeks ongoing consultation until he or she gains more clinical experience.
- A seasoned clinician who initiates and undergoes a course of clinical consultation to respecialize in a particular clinical population or modality of treatment.
- A senior, full-time academician who spends part of his or her sabbatical seeing clients and receiving consultation to stay connected to clinical work.

As one might surmise, the supervision of this spectrum of clinicians is not a case of "one size fits all." The supervisor would have to take into account the supervisee's developmental level (McNeill & Stoltenberg, 2016; see also the Cube Model of competence, Rodolfa et al., 2005) in making the proper assignment of cases (if that is one of the supervisor's functions), deciding the level and intensity of clinical oversight to provide, and evaluating the supervisee's performance and progress. For example, a supervisor may recommend against assigning a high-risk client to a novice therapist in his or her first clinical practicum. If the supervisor does not have administrative input into such case assignments, he or she may then opt to give the inexperienced practicum student extra time and attention in managing the high-risk case. Similarly, the supervisor may be more apt to evaluate the trainee on his or her general level of professionalism in trying to keep the client stable and safe, rather than expecting the supervisee to master advanced techniques, such as guided imagery, in the context of trauma work.

Another example of an adjustment that supervisors may make to evaluate the novice therapist more fairly would be to use the Cognitive Therapy Rating Scale (CTRS; see Chapter 6 for more information) as a checklist of adherence to the treatment model rather than grading each item on its 0–6 competence scale. In this scenario, the inexperienced therapist would only have to incorporate the key elements of CBT into a session (e.g., scoring "yes" or "no" for such items as agenda-setting, collaboration, feedback, homework) rather than perform them at high levels. The CTRS traditionally has not been used in this manner, and we are unaware of any studies that have employed the CTRS without using the scoring system per se, but as a training tool it may be quite useful to introduce the CTRS as an adherence checklist before using it as a scorable competency measure.

As noted, doing a needs assessment addresses the supervisees' developmental level and immediately communicates two positive messages: first, supervisees are respected, involved participants in this partnership called "supervision," and second, the supervisor cares about providing something that is tailor-made. Some of the comments we have heard from supervisees when asked about their training needs include the following:

> "I would like to learn to use some of the specific techniques of CBT, such as thought records, so I can become comfortable with assigning them to clients."

> "I have to admit that I'm a little unsure of myself with the CBT model because I have typically taken a less directive, more Rogerian approach with clients. I want to be able to be more structured and focused but not at the expense of being warm and a good listener. I'm not saying that CBT therapists are not warm and are not good listeners, but I'm not sure how *I'm* going to combine everything. I could use some guidance and feedback in this area."

"I know that this clinic uses video recording a lot, so I'm very interested in getting feedback on my complete sessions and to have the opportunity to see myself on video so I can get a better idea about what I'm doing right and what I need to work on more."

"I really enjoyed my exposure to CBT during residency and think I have a good sense of the theory and basic techniques, but I never did a full course of CBT from start to finish. I'd like to learn how to do that now."

When a trainee is a novice therapist, supervision likely will require significant attention to foundational and functional competencies (Newman, 2010) and thus may include many or all of the following:

- Discussing and practicing rapport-building, listening, and reflection skills.
- Assigning the supervisee basic readings in CBT.
- Psychoeducation (and additional readings) about specific disorders and clinical problems.
- Reviewing the essentials of ethical practice, including discussion of the American Psychological Association (APA) *Ethical Principles of Psychologists and Code of Conduct* (APA, 2002; 2010).
- Presenting an overview of the professional practice of clinical note keeping and the proper use of clinical phone (and other media) contacts.
- Practicing ways to socialize clients into the CBT model.
- Modeling multidisciplinary collaboration and consultation (e.g., contacting and consulting with the client's psychiatrist after receiving authorization from the client).
- Skills practice (e.g., cognitive restructuring, Socratic questioning, graded-task hierarchies, diaphragmatic breathing, guided imagery).
- Beginning a dialogue about cross-cultural factors in doing competent CBT.
- Compiling a list of common CBT homework assignments and their applications.

As trainees advance in their level of understanding of and comfort with cognitive–behavioral theory and techniques, the emphasis in supervision can shift to higher-level therapy competencies, such as case conceptualization, complex techniques with high-risk clients, and recognizing and repairing strains in the therapeutic relationship.

The American Psychological Association (Fouad et al., 2009) has developed functional competency benchmarks that may serve as a useful aid for the supervisor to evaluate his or her trainees' skill set relative to their level of training and professional development. Although not specific to development as a cognitive–behavioral therapist, the benchmarks identify 16 key domains (including professionalism, scientific knowledge and methods, and evidence-based practice) across which trainees' progress toward independent practice can be evaluated. Each domain comprises behavioral anchors suggesting a trainee's readiness for practicum, internship, and entry to practice, respectively. The benchmarks may serve as a useful aid to the supervisor in setting goals for a training year that are appropriate to a trainee's developmental level and evaluating psychology trainees' progress toward the goals as the year progresses. Benchmarks pertinent to the behaviors of the supervisors themselves also have been developed (Falender & Shafranske, in press).

Supervisors working with psychiatry residents may wish to familiarize themselves with the Psychiatry Milestone Project, an initiative that was jointly developed through the Accreditation Council for Graduate Medical Education (ACGME) and the American Board of Psychiatry and Neurology (2014). Similar to the benchmarks described, the psychiatry milestones identify key areas of competency across inpatient and outpatient psychiatry, consultation, and psychotherapy supervision. For supervisors interested in CBT-specific measures of competency to aid in goal setting and evaluation, the ACGME (2001) also has developed guidelines for psychiatry resident competency in CBT. These include the ability to formulate clients' diagnoses according to a CBT model, structuring sessions for maximal effectiveness, helping clients identify and modify unhelpful cognitions, and developing a strong and active therapeutic alliance (also see Friedberg, Mahr, & Mahr, 2010; Kamholz, Liverant, Black, Aaronson, & Hill, 2014; Sudak, 2009; Sudak, Beck, & Wright, 2003).

Now let us examine the issue of how the methods of clinical supervision are influenced by the particular training setting. In settings such as a university-based clinic, in which the therapist-in-training is an advanced-degree candidate and the supervisor is one of the faculty, the supervisor's jurisdiction over the course of a client's treatment and the nature of supervision are generally clear. In other contexts, the role of the clinical supervisor and the course of treatment may be dependent in part on factors outside the context of the supervisory relationship. The following examples (adapted from Belar, 2008) highlight some of the factors that may influence a supervisor's role, responsibilities, and structuring of supervision:

- The supervisor would prefer that the trainee audiotape or videotape sessions, but the setting in which the trainee is working does not allow the recording of sessions owing to concerns about confidentiality.
- Agency charting and documentation requirements compel trainees to file a client contact note within 24 hours of the corresponding therapy session, which does not allow sufficient time for the supervisor to review or edit the note before its official entry.
- A practicum student on a psycho-oncology service sees her client for individual therapy sessions at bedside and accompanies him to a chemotherapy session multiple times within the course of a week; thus, several treatment contacts occur between supervision sessions, which the supervisor may find potentially problematic.
- A trainee working as part of a multidisciplinary team on a psychiatric inpatient unit is given direction and input regarding the course of treatment by team members and providers other than the primary supervisor, some of whom share legal responsibility for the client's welfare.
- A psychologist serves as the CBT supervisor for a psychiatry resident who also discusses her clients regularly with a psychopharmacology supervisor and the medical director of the outpatient clinic in which the clients are seen.

In situations such as those outlined, the familiar model of weekly supervision in the supervisor's office may not match the demands of the agency or the client population. The concept of "flexibility within fidelity" (Kendall et al., 2008), generally used to refer to the dissemination and implementation of evidence-based therapy in real-world clinical settings, may be a helpful model for conceptualizing the selection and application of best practices in supervision across a variety of settings and client populations. For example, a supervisor who is accustomed to reviewing audiotapes of therapy sessions may be unable to do so if a trainee is providing services on an inpatient unit that does not allow client recordings. In such cases, the supervisor may request to observe a session from behind a one-way mirror with the client's consent or sit in on an entire therapy session (i.e., supervision cotherapy) to obtain the firsthand information that ordinarily would be gleaned through audiotape or video review. When the supervisor does not go to the training site and therefore cannot directly observe the supervisee's work, the supervisee can be encouraged to take copious notes (including direct quotes from both the client and the supervisee) during and immediately after a session. Although not as comprehensive and veridical as a recording or a live observation, such extradetailed note taking may be enough to provide transcriptionlike material for review in supervision.

DOCUMENTATION

Supervisors are responsible for impressing upon their trainees the necessity of keeping good, thorough clinical notes on each case. Whether the notes are written in a physical chart or in a formal, protected electronic system, the supervisor also must review and cosign the trainee's notes. Both the notes themselves and the supervisor's cosignatures must be done in a timely fashion. Such documentation is vital for medical–legal purposes, serves a training function, and provides the supervisor with a measure of the trainee's clinical thinking style.

The contents of clinical notes ideally contain the following information:

- Personal identifiers, including the name and date of birth (and perhaps medical record number) of the client and the name of the therapist and supervisor.
- The client's diagnosis and/or other concrete description of the clinical problem(s).
- Data from client self-report measures (e.g., the Beck Depression Inventory II, Beck, Steer, & Brown, 1996; the Outcome Questionnaire,

Lambert, Lunnen, Umphress, Hansen, & Burlingame, 1994; The Patient Health Questionnaire-9, Kroenke, Spitzer, & Williams, 2001), or from interview-based or observational measures (e.g., the Beck Scale for Suicide Ideation, Beck, Kovacs, & Weissman, 1979).

- A brief mental status checklist.
- A risk-assessment checklist (e.g., presence or absence of suicidal ideation, intent, plan).
- An agenda for the session, as well as a list of ongoing goals.
- The body of the note itself, including problems that were identified and addressed, the interventions that were used, the main "teaching points" of the session for the client, homework that was reviewed and/ or assigned, important quotes from the client and/or the therapist, and the client's level of responsiveness and progress in the session.
- Signatures (or e-signatures) of the therapist and supervisor, the date of today's session, and the date of the next appointment (if applicable).

As one can see, writing notes that are this thorough requires the trainee to be efficient, industrious, conscientious, professionally accountable, and clinically astute. As such, trainees' notes are an excellent barometer of their ascending competence.

Effective supervisors routinely read the trainees' written accounts of their interactions with clients (e.g., assessments, therapy sessions, clinically relevant telephone contacts) to offer feedback, suggest changes, and sign the notes. Supervisors can be role models for good record keeping by keeping their own supervision notes and adding commentaries to the trainees' charts when they (the supervisors) have contact with the clients, such as when they sit in for part or all of a session, speak with the client directly by phone, or intervene in the care of the client in a crisis situation (as described later).

When supervisors carefully evaluate the contents of their supervisees' clinical notes, valuable teaching points may emerge. The following are sample comments from supervisors, in which they give feedback to the supervisees about their documentation of their work with clients:

> "I'm glad to hear that you called your client the day after your previous session to see how he was doing and to get an update on his level of suicidal thinking. Please create a note for that in the chart. Writing a

note will show that you are following through with the treatment plan of giving this client extra safety monitoring on an outpatient basis."

"Did your client fill out her mood inventories last session? The note didn't contain her scores. If she declined to do them, insert a comment to that effect. If possible, ask her to come a little bit early to sessions so she can complete these questionnaires. It would be great to keep a running tabulation of her scores as one of the measures of her progress."

"I think you have a good rationale for postponing the exposure intervention with this client. He seems to be ambivalent about being in CBT, and if you push this intervention it may lead to his leaving therapy before you really get a chance to help him. Add a comment about this rationale in the clinical note. We want the chart to reflect your clinical thinking behind the decision to include or not include a particular intervention."

"It's a pleasure to review your session notes! They're well-written, clear, thorough, and really give a sense that you have conceptualized your clients well. Excellent! I know it's time-intensive to do this, but I hope you'll keep up this great work."

INSTRUCTION, MODELING, ROLE-PLAYING, AND REVIEWING RECORDINGS

Effective CBS, similar to effective CBT, involves collaboration between the participants such that both parties are actively working. In supervision, the "work" often involves the supervisors offering instructions and demonstrations about how to properly interact with clients in various clinical situations, using a range of CBT methods, whereas the supervisees answer questions, explain their treatment plans, generate hypotheses, and practice procedures (e.g., via role-playing with the supervisor). Competent supervisors strive for this sort of balance of effort, such that the trainees gradually learn to think independently, and the supervisors guide and shape them with well-crafted questions, comments, instructions, and examples of "how to do x." Clearly, an important part of gaining and maintaining such supervisory skills includes being (and staying) competent in delivering CBT as a therapist. In the following sample dialogue, a CBT supervisor guides her supervisee to elicit more specific information from a client whose communication style is vague and avoidant.

Trainee: I've found that it's very hard work to try to understand my client. I try to ask the right questions, but he's very slippery, if that's an appropriate term to use. He talks a lot, but I really have trouble following him, and then I don't quite know what to do when he looks at me and asks, "Do you understand?" because a lot of the time I really don't know what he's talking about, and I'm hesitant to say that.

Supervisor: Tell me about your hesitation, if you don't mind. What do you think it would mean, and what do you think would happen if you told him that you would like to understand him better, but that sometimes it's difficult to follow him?

Trainee: I guess I have two concerns. One is that I don't want to seem like I'm not listening, and the other concern is that I don't want to imply that he's not making sense.

Supervisor: Fair enough. How can you tell him in a way that mitigates those concerns?

Trainee: I could just be honest and say, "I'm sorry, but I don't understand, and I really want to understand, so could you clarify that for me again?"

Supervisor: Absolutely. Keep it simple, humble, and honest. Sometimes you just have to give the clients some differential reinforcement so they know where they stand. If they're communicating clearly, and you respond in a way that shows that you're 'getting it,' then your response reinforces their clear communication. Conversely, if you tell the clients that you need them to clarify further, then that gives them feedback that they need to modify how they're explaining things. If you do this in a polite, caring, manner—as I know that you can—this might be all you need to do.

Trainee: That makes sense, but I often worry that this client is going to be annoyed at me if I say this, or maybe he won't be capable of explaining things better, and he will just get frustrated.

Supervisor: That could happen. If the client did respond to your polite, caring request with annoyance and frustration, what clinical data would that provide you?

Trainee: I would hypothesize that he is very sensitive to being mis-understood, perhaps because that happens a lot in his life. Another related hypothesis might be that he is misinterpreting my comment as being an accusation or an insult. That could be reflective of a "mistrust" schema, or maybe it could be an "incompetency" schema if he's upset with himself for struggling to make himself understood.

Supervisor: All of those are useful hypotheses. Well done! I hope that he will respond well to your entreaties, but if he gets flustered in the way that you anticipate he will, you will gain valuable material for hypothesis generation and hypothesis testing.

A week later, this same supervisor–trainee dyad reviewed an audio recording that the trainee made of one of her sessions with the client discussed previously. Their dialogue about the case continues here:

Supervisor: In listening to this session, I can see why it's difficult to communicate with this client. I notice that he uses a lot of pronouns, but he rarely spells out what the corresponding noun is. He says things like, "*This* isn't what I want," "*That* doesn't work for me," and, "Can I ever make *it* better?" Maybe you can ask him for the nouns that go with "this," "that," and "it."

Trainee: Asking him for more nouns might be a little awkward, but I'll try.

Supervisor: Well, it's "awkward" if we're talking about a conversation in everyday life, but this is therapy, where "awkward" is part of the territory! I don't mean to make light of this, mind you. You can be very nice about it, saying, "When you tell me that '*This* is not what I want,' what exactly are you referring to by '*this?*'"

Trainee: Okay, I'll try to ask him for the nouns.

Supervisor: I also noticed something else about the client's style and yours, too.

Trainee: Oh? I'm curious.

Supervisor: You asked the client some really good open-ended questions. Very thought-provoking questions indeed. As I listened to the recording, I eagerly awaited the client's answers, but they never came. He skated right around your questions. It's quite a consistent pattern. It's almost like you're not having a dialogue. You ask a question, and he talks about something else. You follow him and ask another good question that relates to what he's talking about now, and he replies about something else yet again. It goes on and on like that. He's a moving target.

Trainee: I hadn't thought about it like that before, but I think you're right. His style of avoiding my questions is part of the reason I'm not connecting with him, and why I'm not "getting" him. Do you think that's deliberate on his part? Is he purposely avoiding my questions?

Supervisor: That could be part of his overall avoidant style. Or maybe he's not really hearing you. Or maybe he hears you all too well and doesn't want to answer. You can explore this by returning to your original question, rather than letting the client take you on a wild goose chase.

Trainee: You mean, just say to him, "Could we get back to the earlier question? I am interested in hearing your thoughts."

Supervisor: Exactly. Try asking him again. Bring him back to the question you asked.

Trainee: I might get more useful information from the client that way, and maybe I will understand him better. On the other hand, I might find that he doesn't take kindly to my probing. Either way, we'll go beyond our current stuck point.

Supervisor: Well put! I agree. Let's see what happens next session.

If the trainee records the following session and the supervisor listens to it, the supervisor will be able to hear the extent to which the trainee was able to follow through with the plan to nicely ask the client to be more specific about what he means and to return to the original questions that seemed to get lost in the shuffle. Indeed, this is one of the many advantages of making recordings—the supervisor can ascertain how much "transfer" there is from the supervision session to the therapy session and to what degree this facilitated a productive response from the client.

When reviewing recordings of supervisees' sessions with clients, supervisors can offer feedback on a moment-to-moment basis (such as when segments of the session are played and then paused for discussion) or more global feedback with regard to the entirety of the session. Both of these approaches have utility, although they each pose their own challenges. For example, moment-to-moment feedback can be helpful in elucidating clinical choice points, such as when the supervisees are asked why they responded to their clients in one way versus another and how they interpreted their clients' comments and other behaviors at the moments they occurred. On the downside, an overzealous supervisor can micromanage a supervisee, suggesting too many options and offering too much critical feedback without first seeing how the session progressed. Such an approach is to be avoided if possible because it can foment trainee self-doubt and increase trainee self-consciousness (when, instead, they need to be most conscious of the client!). An effective CBT supervisor understands and communicates that there often are many "correct" ways to run a session and that the trainee does not necessarily have to mimic exactly what the supervisor thinks he or she might have done at that precise moment on the recording. Given that metaphors can be quite helpful in the process of learning for clients and supervisees alike (Edwards, 2010; Stott, Mansell, Salkovskis, Lavender, & Cartwright-Hatton, 2010), the supervisor's comment that follows includes a metaphor to make this point:

Supervisor: Conducting an effective CBT session is like climbing a tree. The goal is to get to the top, and although it clearly takes the right set of skills and mental "mapping" to get there, it is probably true that there are many different "branch combinations" that one could take to achieve the goal. I might take one particular route to climb the tree, and you might take another, and we may both wind up succeeding and meeting at the top. The key is in having a plan and being flexible enough to alter the plan if one route seems too risky or if the originally chosen path seems unlikely to take you to the top. The more you know about CBT conceptualization and interventions, the more branches you will have to choose from, and the stronger the therapeutic relationship is, the sturdier the branches will be, allowing you more leeway to find your way safely, even with a mistake or two along the way. So when I tell you that I might say or do something different than what you said or did in the recording, I'm not saying that you were incorrect or that my way is better. I'm just encouraging you to see how there may be more than one way to accomplish your goals and that you don't have to be overly worried and self-conscious about doing everything right at all times or only in a particular way.

On the other hand, there may be discrete sections in a supervisee's recorded session on which a supervisor would like to focus to provide a valuable teaching moment. For example, the supervisor may wish to suggest a particular intervention at a particular point in time, such as by advising the supervisee to nicely ask the client what is going through her mind when she demonstrates a marked shift in affect (e.g., she stops talking in midsentence and looks away) or suggesting that the supervisee ask the client, "What constructive action can you take to begin to deal with this problem?" when the client needs some practice in implementing problem-solving methods. In the following example, the supervisor hones in on a specific comment the supervisee made to his client. The goal is to help the supervisee to be more empathic and effective with a client whose expressions of anger were interfering with the therapeutic dialogue in session.

Trainee: I know I didn't handle this session well. I felt a bit helpless in the face of my client's anger. She was bitterly complaining about so many things, and she seemed to be escalating, to the point where I couldn't complete a sentence without her interrupting me. I remember thinking that this was an example of a "therapy-interfering behavior," but I wasn't sure how to address it.

Supervisor: I've been there myself, so I understand what you mean by saying that you felt "helpless." I appreciate the fact that you're willing to talk about what didn't go very well in your session. That takes a lot of courage and trust in the supervision process. It also shows me that you're interested in learning, even when it hurts!

Trainee: Thanks. I definitely want to figure out what I can do differently when a client is so emotionally dysregulated like that.

Supervisor: I can offer two points right away. One is a general comment. The other is very specific, having to do with something you said to your client that I think you can change in the future. The general comment is that a client's therapy-interfering behaviors provide you with valuable information that can be conceptualized. Therefore, rather than just feeling "helpless," you can be thinking that you will use this adverse incident in session to understand your client a little better. You may not be able to say an entire sentence without being interrupted, but you can silently conceptualize and hypothesize what is going on, and this is not being "helpless."

Trainee: That's very helpful. If I think about conceptualizing, I might not feel so at a loss about what to do, and it might help me to know what to say at a different time, when the client is not so emotionally activated. What was the specific comment I said that I should change?

Supervisor: First, I want to say that you're making a good point about how conceptualizing helps you to know what to say—whether it's now or later—in order to have the best chance of intervening empathically and constructively. That's great that you're getting that point. We'll talk much more about that later. But here's the comment that you made that I think you can change. There was a moment when you said to your client, "I need you to calm down right now."

Trainee: Oh, that was terrible! It's not about what *I* need. After I said that she just got worse.

Supervisor: Nice catch. You already get it. Good self-observation.

Trainee: I think I said it out of desperation. I was thinking that if I just sat there passively she would continue to escalate, and that wouldn't be helpful. But I didn't necessarily know what to say either. So I blurted out the comment, "I need you to calm down right now," which I regret.

Supervisor: Even though there's no magic formula for getting a client to de-escalate on the spot, there is a middle ground between being passive and helpless on the one extreme, and saying something potentially unempathic or confrontational on the other extreme. For example, rather than saying that you need for her to calm down right now, you can *behave* in such a way that it will gradually help her to feel understood, and perhaps that will help her "calm down" gradually.

Trainee: That's what I wanted to do. I tried to be a good listener, but that seemed so inadequate.

Supervisor: Well, being a good listener is a pretty good start. Also, you can physically lean in a bit, showing that you are very attentive, with a somber, sympathetic facial expression, and you can add simple, soft-spoken phrases that might not get interrupted, such as, "I'm listening," or "I hear you," or "That's so hard," or "I'm with you," and other comments like that. Then you're less likely to be perceived by your client as demanding that she be quiet, or that she's bothering you, or that you're telling her she doesn't have a right to her feelings, and you're more likely to be perceived as someone who is trying to be there. That might assist the process of her de-escalating, and later—when the timing is better—you can talk more about what she was perceiving at that moment, and how she could regulate her emotions more effectively.

In the example given, the supervisor used a specific moment in a session recording to give the supervisee some corrective feedback. This included suggesting methods that potentially could be used effectively across similar situations in the future in which a client is emotionally dysregulated and the therapist wants to find a happy medium between being passive and engaging in a power struggle. The supervisor also gives positive reinforcement for the supervisee's ability to self-reflect and self-correct, which in turn positively reinforces the supervisory relationship and promotes supervisee learning.

With regard to giving feedback on an entire session, perhaps including the use of a measure such as the original or revised version of the CTRS (Blackburn et al., 2001; Young & Beck, 1980), the benefits include being able to see how the supervisee plans, organizes, and constructs a full session. The supervisor can see how well the supervisee stays on task and yet shifts gears if unexpected, relevant clinical information comes to light. Similarly, the supervisor can ascertain whether the supervisee creates a therapeutic atmosphere in which the client feels both supported and encouraged to work toward change. The supervisor can also determine if the homework assignment grows out of what has been discussed in the session and if the supervisee is providing the client with opportunities to practice skills and provide feedback. On the downside, it is often impractical to review previously unseen recordings of entire therapy sessions within the scope of a single supervision session. More often, the supervisor needs to take the extra time to review (and perhaps rate) the recording on his or her own time and then use part of the next supervision session to offer feedback and encourage discussion.

The CTRS can also serve as an *interrater reliability check* of sorts. This is when the supervisor asks the supervisee to choose one of the latter's recorded sessions, and then they both rate the session independently. They then compare their respective ratings, which can be an extremely instructive exercise. Supervisors can gain a glimpse at how the supervisees assess their own skills, and both parties can share their rationales about why they rated each item of the CTRS the way they did. Admittedly, our suggested reliability check in this instance is more for clinical training than for statistical or psychometric purposes.

It should be acknowledged that recording supervisees' sessions and observing them—similar to engaging in role-playing exercises in supervision—has the potential to provoke anxiety in supervisees. Supervisors need to be mindful of this and be suitably empathic. In our experience, the pros of recording supervisees' sessions for evaluation far outweigh the cons. In citing the literature on this subject, Nelson (2014) states that the evidence suggests that few therapists-in-training actually have problems with making recordings and that those who experience some anxiety at first typically succeed in adapting with repetition (as one might expect based on the principles of habituation). Supervisors themselves can serve as effective coping models by showing the recordings of their own unedited CBT sessions with clients. Supervisors who are willing to display their own imperfect work, perhaps offering self-supervisory advice along the way (e.g., "If I could go back and do this session again, I would have said . . .") contribute to a sense of collaboration and congruence in supervision.

SUPERVISION INDIVIDUALLY OR IN A GROUP

At times the CBT supervisor may have a choice between structuring supervision individually or in a small-group format. Individual supervision allows for more in-depth discussion of fewer clients and a supervisory experience that may be more tailored to the individual supervisee's learning needs. When supervisees are working with clients who are at high risk or have complex needs, individual supervision may be necessary to devote sufficient time to case conceptualization and thorough treatment planning. Individual supervision may also be preferable when supervisees are in need of remediation of foundational competencies or additional training in a specific area of CBT. The time required to help supervisees achieve the desired level of competence combined with the supervisee's right to discretion about the need for remediation together suggest that supervision in these instances might best be conducted on a one-to-one basis. Similarly, any significant areas of conflict between supervisor and supervisee generally are best addressed within the context of individual supervision.

Small-group supervision (sessions of which may need to be longer than an hour, if feasible) can provide increased opportunities to learn cognitive–behavioral theory and technique through exposure to cohorts' case presentations. With more than one supervisee present, there are ample opportunities to enhance supervision with role-playing, skills practice in a group format, and modeling of CBT techniques. The decision to provide CBS in a group format requires the supervisor to be especially mindful of triaging and agenda setting. A formal agenda for supervision set at the beginning of each session is necessary to ensure that risk levels are adequately assessed for each client under supervision, that the most critical issues are addressed, and that each trainee gets sufficient time for discussion and feedback.

Particularly for more advanced supervisees, group or dyadic supervision may be a useful arena for fostering their own development as clinical supervisors. Over the course of a supervisory hour, the participants can be encouraged to share their own insights and suggestions on each other's cases, thereby honing their "supervisory ear" and their therapeutic one. Small-group and dyadic supervision also provides an opportunity for more formalized practice of supervisory skills. For example, trainees can alternate in taking on the role of a supervisor, in which they facilitate agenda setting for the session, help each other to work through stuck points in a recent therapy session, and set goals for the next session. In such a situation the clinical supervisor effectively plays the role of *metasupervisor* (Newman, 2013), providing feedback to the trainees not only on their work as therapists but also on their effectiveness and areas for development as a future supervisor.

Practice in the supervisory role can at times be introduced even with trainees who are less experienced with the CBT model. For example, one of us (DK) teaches an introductory CBT course for third-year psychiatry residents. New course material frequently is introduced by having the residents divide into groups of three, with each group member having the chance to play the role of client, therapist, or observer at different times. As each new skill—for example, agenda setting or completing a thought record—is introduced, the triad has the opportunity to practice it in vivo, with the observer providing feedback to the therapist on his or her ability to explain concepts clearly and apply them effectively in working with the client.

Regardless of the level of CBT-specific experience of the trainees in a group supervision format, it is important for the supervisor to summarize overtly and reinforce the most important teaching points of their meetings. In this way, the supervisor serves as an editor-in-chief of sorts so that the lessons learned can be distilled into their most valid components and instilled in the group's supervisees via repetition and the supervisor's confirmatory comments.

3

Structure and Process of Supervision

The purpose of this chapter is to describe a typical routine that a cognitive–behavioral therapy (CBT) supervisor and supervisee generally will follow for time efficiency, breadth of coverage of relevant clinical material, and optimization of learning. As will become apparent in the case illustration provided (taken from *Cognitive–Behavioral Therapy Supervision*, the companion DVD to this volume),[1] the evidence-based supervisor takes a multimodal approach (see Milne, 2009). Using methods such as didactics, Socratic questions, measures of progress (both the clients' and the supervisee's), audiovisual recordings, modeling, role-playing, and other methods, the supervisor instills and enhances learning through multiple channels of perception and enactment.

---

[1] *Cognitive–Behavioral Therapy Supervision*, available from APA Books at http://www.apa.org/pubs/videos/4310957.aspx.

http://dx.doi.org/10.1037/14950-004
Supervision Essentials for Cognitive–Behavioral Therapy, by C. F. Newman and D. A. Kaplan

WHAT HAPPENS IN THE SUPERVISION SESSIONS?

The CBT supervisor sets an agenda at the start of a supervision meeting, similar to the way a therapist structures a therapy session. The well-being of the supervisee's clients is the top priority; therefore, a review of each of the cases generally takes top billing. The specific order of review of the cases depends on the number of clients who need to be covered and their respective levels of severity and/or urgency. A well-managed agenda allows the supervisor–supervisee dyad to give the proper amount of attention to each case.

Aside from review of each case (and corresponding clinical notes), the supervision meeting agenda may include general topics pertinent to the delivery of CBT, such as properly applying certain techniques (e.g., thought records, exposure hierarchies, relaxation inductions, imagery work, modifying core beliefs), constructing a case conceptualization, designing homework in ways that will be most helpful for the clients (and most likely to earn their collaboration), and managing strains in the therapeutic relationship. Similarly (time permitting), the supervision meeting may involve informative discussions about such topics as the common characteristics of clients with particular diagnoses (e.g., eating disorders, posttraumatic stress disorder, personality disorders), or about issues pertinent to phase of treatment (e.g., the proper handling of termination and transfer). Additional important topics that may find their way onto the agenda include ethical questions and cross-cultural matters in treatment. Ideally, these would be brought up in the context of one or more of the cases being supervised, but they may be discussed as freestanding topics.

As noted, supervision sessions may include experiential exercises (e.g., role-playing) and/or listening to (or viewing) recordings of the supervisee's recent work with a given client. Of course, the supervisor will have confirmed that the client has given consent to the recording, understands that the recording will be used in clinical supervision, and knows the parameters for its further use in training or prompt deletion. Supervisors make sure that the supervisees tell their clients that the latter are free to say "no" to being recorded and that the clients continue to receive the level of attention and treatment they expect. At the same time, some initially reluctant clients eventually give consent when they are told that by being recorded for supervision they are receiving an extra high level of consultation on their case and that it is their *therapist* who is being evaluated, not them (the clients). The agenda of a cognitive–behavioral supervision (CBS) meeting may also include didactic instruction (e.g., discussing assigned readings, reviewing different methods for teaching clients self-help techniques), handling clinical dilemmas, and working on treatment plans. Supervisors and their supervisees collaboratively decide how to apportion the time that will be devoted to these myriad topics, and the supervisor models being a good manager of time.

There may be times when there is little new clinical material to review in a supervision session (e.g., following a time of the year when therapists and clients alike have been on vacation and sessions have been temporarily put on hold). Rather than canceling a supervision session at such times, it may be better to take advantage of the situation by doing alternative training activities, such as the supervisor showing an old video of his or her own work with a client, or engaging in role-play exercises to provide the supervisee with valuable practice. Far from just filling time when there are no clients to discuss, doing experiential exercises is indispensable when teaching trainees the complexities of conducting CBT (Ronen & Rosenbaum, 1998).

CASE ILLUSTRATION

Let us talk a bit about "what happens in a supervision session," as depicted in the video of the supervision session of one of us (CN) with his supervisee, an advanced graduate student (Andrew). We will start with a general overview, followed by a section on the supervisor's thoughts at specific moments.

General Overview of the Four Agenda Items

The supervision session was roughly divided into a four-part agenda that was collaboratively set up during the first few minutes of the meeting. Most of the contents and structure of this supervision session were typical of such meetings, although the reviewing of Andrew's recorded session with his client "G" and its scoring with the Cognitive Therapy Rating Scale (CTRS; Young & Beck, 1980) represented a "special" occurrence; such reviews were done three times during the semester. Given that there were no emergent issues involving a high-risk client in immediate need, this recorded session (and its rating) was placed at the top of the agenda. After that was another "special" topic, the reviewing of Andrew's final session with his client "S," including the way the termination note provided an overview of the work that had been done in S's course of treatment, his current condition, and his maintenance plan for continuing to use his CBT self-skills going forward. The next agenda item focused on an African-American client, but rather than reviewing a recent therapy session per se the supervisor and supervisee addressed the way the client's ethnic/cultural background played an important role with regard to the therapeutic relationship and the treatment plan. Finally, the fourth agenda item centered on an ethical issue Andrew needed to confront in response to a client's strong request that he become her sister's individual therapist. The supervisor helped Andrew to frame the ethical dilemma, to freely express his discomfort, and to try to see more than one side to the issue so as not to allow his discomfort be the only consideration in making a decision about how best to handle the matter. Finally, the supervisor engaged Andrew in a role-play to help him work on a repertoire for nicely saying "no" to the client, being able to manage any sort of alliance strain that might occur as a result of saying no, and doing some constructive problem solving with the client rather than just letting the matter come to a screeching halt when Andrew said "no."

The supervision session was densely packed with useful clinical material, which is one of the benefits of structuring the meeting by using an agenda at the start. Case material was reviewed, not merely to check on the current status of the clients (although that is important) but also to plan strategy for upcoming sessions. The supervisor offered several hypotheses and suggestions but also occasionally asked the supervisee what he thought he could do next in his treatment of a given client, thus encouraging Andrew to do some independent problem solving rather than simply instructing him on what to do (see Cummings, Ballantyne,

& Scallion, 2015). The supervisor offered positive feedback and constructive criticism within the context of a congenial, collaborative supervisory relationship, as summarized in Exhibit 3.1.

The supervision session was also noteworthy for its use of a role-play exercise to help the supervisee practice benevolently setting a limit with a client, a valuable skill for a trainee who needs to learn the delicate balance between asserting professional authority and maintaining a sense of respectful collaboration. The supervision meeting also addressed a sensitive cross-cultural issue, in that a client had experienced racial discrimination that the supervisor and Andrew (as "two white guys") needed to

---

Exhibit 3.1

Positive Feedback and Constructive Criticism in the Supervision Session

Positive feedback: The supervisor noted that the supervisee ...

- Conducted a session with G that was scored at well above the acknowledged level of competency as indicated on the CTRS.
- Had a particularly strong therapeutic relationship with G and that his strategy for change—involving multiple methods such as cognitive restructuring, current behavioral exposures to avoided situations, processing of past trauma, and client skill-building (e.g., communication with her son)—was on target and had the potential to effect significant therapeutic change.
- Helped his client S attain remarkable changes over the course of treatment, far more than the supervisor had expected in light of the deficits that the client showed at intake.
- Wrote very good clinical notes and the supervisor (in his role as cosigner) appreciated this.
- Used methods from dialectical behavior therapy and acceptance and commitment therapy that the supervisor found educational, and therefore was grateful for learning from the supervisee.

(continued)

Exhibit 3.1

**Positive Feedback and Constructive Criticism
in the Supervision Session (*Continued*)**

- Had shown excellent self-awareness in recognizing that his client G had "pushed his buttons" with regard to how she interacted with her son. Notably, instead of simply acting on this feeling and telling the client not to treat her son that way, Andrew recognized that he had to process his reaction silently while staying focused on the client's needs.
- Did the right thing in deferring giving an answer to the client who wanted him to become the individual therapist for her sister, instead saying that he would have to consult with his supervisor. The supervisor stated that this is good practice when confronted with an ethical gray zone.

Constructive criticism: The supervisor added that the supervisee . . .

- Had uncharacteristically chosen not to give client G an overt homework assignment. However, the supervisor stated that Andrew had been giving the client "implied," ongoing assignments, such as showing up at work despite her being anxious. Therefore, homework was not being neglected entirely. Nevertheless, the supervisor advised Andrew to make the homework assignments more explicit, so that there would be no misunderstanding going forward.
- Could broaden the scope of his clinical thinking by giving consideration to the "devil's advocate" position of saying "yes" to his client's request to provide therapy to her sister. In other words, instead of simply allowing the state of "feeling uncomfortable" with the client's request to dictate his answer, Andrew could more thoroughly consider the pros, the cons, and the contextual factors relevant to this ethical gray-zone situation.

acknowledge humbly that they might not adequately be able to comprehend at a personal level (see Falender, Shafranske, & Falicov, 2014).

Another important moment occurred when the supervisor advised Andrew that it was not necessary for him to disclose too much of his own personal information in supervision to deal effectively with an emotional reaction to a client. This is an example of the boundary between providing supervision and providing therapy. The supervisor stated that it was important for Andrew to use his personal reactions as a "cue" that he needed to stay focused on the client and not let his own feelings unduly guide his choice of intervention. In this particular supervisory session, the supervisor was satisfied that Andrew was able to process his own reactions appropriately. If there had been evidence to the contrary, the supervisor might have asked Andrew to do some self-help assignments to improve his self-reflection and self-practice, perhaps by using the Bennett-Levy, Thwaites, Haarhoff, and Perry (2015) workbook. For example, Andrew could do the exercise that asks therapists to write about a personal pattern that may be impinging on their work with a particular client (p. 118) and then to write about what they learned about themselves as a result of working on a problem-solving diagram (p. 135).

Specific Moments/The Supervisor's Thoughts

In setting the agenda, I (CN) wanted to devote much of the time to the case of G given that I had listened to an entire session recording. However, I first checked in with Andrew to make sure that there were no pressing matters (e.g., high-risk situations with other clients) that would require a lot of time. I also wanted to leave sufficient time to discuss other agenda items of import. Once we reached a collaborative agreement (within the first 5 minutes of the supervision session), I summarized the four items on our agenda and we proceeded.

1. *Client G*: I thanked Andrew for providing me with a CD of his audio-recorded session with G. This meant that the session was not transmitted to me online, and therefore confidential material easily could be contained and disposed. I told Andrew that he performed well on

the CTRS, and I summarized some of the activities I had heard that signified a competently conducted CBT session. Although I did not spend time reviewing the scoring code item by item, I told Andrew that his score was well above the acknowledged competency cutoff score of 40 (for a more complete discussion of the history and parameters of CTRS scoring, see McManus, Rakovshik, Kennerley, Fennell, & Westbrook, 2012; Muse & McManus, 2013). I advised Andrew to be more explicit about assigning G a homework assignment (which would give Andrew a higher CTRS score), although I acknowledged that G's success in going to work every day was itself an extension of previous homework assignments involving between-session exposure to feared and avoided situations. Andrew and I talked about G's fear of talking to her son about his suicidal ideation combined with her intrusive "helicopter parent" behaviors. Andrew used the case conceptualization to explain that G lamented that she had not been able to "save" her mother from suicide many years ago, and now she was trying to protect her son from the threat of suicide by hovering and trying to manage his mood. Unfortunately, she also maintained a problematic belief that bringing up the subject of suicide with the son could actually precipitate his making an attempt. Thus, Andrew and I concluded that it would be useful for him to discuss this belief with G and to use role-playing to help her practice how she could communicate her concerns effectively and safely to her son. At the same time, I noted that G was understandably frightened by her son's suicidality and that we would have to respect her right to say "no" if she could not be persuaded about the potential benefits of talking openly with her son. In a good example of the division between "teaching and treating," I applauded Andrew's citing his personal reaction to G's behavior toward her son so that he could remain as objective as possible in giving her feedback that fit *her* life situation. In other words, he spotted his "countertransference" reaction, and in being self-aware he was able to stay on task. As befits the behavior of a CBT supervisor, I did not pursue the matter further because I was satisfied that Andrew's self-awareness was a sufficient safeguard in this situation. I made it clear to Andrew that he did not need to tell me more of the details of his personal history that would account for his internal reaction. If I had believed that he was not sufficiently self-aware, I might have given him an assignment to self-explore on his own time and ask him for his conclusions about how best to proceed with the client, keeping his personal response to the side.

2. *The termination session and written summary on client S:* We reflected on Andrew's successful treatment of S, who began therapy as a highly avoidant young man with significant deficits in social functioning. Now, at termination, S not only had low scores on his Beck inventories (signifying few mood symptoms), he was actively dating, and he was more willing to recognize and acknowledge the full spectrum of his emotions. I was pleased that Andrew had promptly completed the written termination summary for this case, an important aspect of case documentation. I also gave Andrew kudos for his idea of having S hold CBT self-help sessions (after therapy) at home as a way of practicing his skills and therefore improving the chances of maintaining his gains. Andrew and I briefly summarized the case conceptualization and related techniques as a way to remind ourselves of the route that had been taken to help this client overcome his fears of his own thoughts and feelings (based on being frightened of the thoughts and feelings of his estranged father, who was severely mentally ill). With Andrew's support of S and effective management of his treatment plan, S exceeded my expectations of what he would gain from therapy, and I let Andrew know how praiseworthy this was.

3. *The special cross-cultural issue with the "I.T. Guy":* Before talking about our third agenda item, I did a clock check with Andrew as a way of confirming that we had sufficient time to devote to the remaining items on our supervision list for today. We then focused on the "I.T. Guy," an African-American male client who seemed to be living the American dream of a high-level job and financial success but who was chronically angry, in part as a result of his personal experiences with racial injustice. Andrew astutely noted that the client had suffered grievously from his father's incarceration, adding that the client believed that a white

person would not have been imprisoned for a similar offense. Andrew and I had to ponder our conundrum of trying to help the client manage his anger without implying that his anger was without just cause, especially as we ("two white guys") were not in a position to know how he felt. I hit upon the idea of asking Andrew to give the client a homework assignment in which he would research historic quotes from famous people of color (male and female) who wrote about dealing with racial injustice in part through strength of mind-set. In this way, we could suggest that the client had a right to rail against the system that jailed his father and still could use his personal skills to be the master of his moods. I added that perhaps Andrew and I could offer to learn from the client by being willing to read something (that the client would recommend to us for our own homework) so that we could be his "students" on this cross-cultural topic. To his credit, Andrew was tactful and careful about taking my suggestion, saying that he would "run it by the client first." This was exactly the right thing to do since it might be presumptuous of me to ask the client to be our teacher when he is expecting us to help him; he might not want to be put in the position of having to educate us. The client should make the call on this one. We just want to communicate that we are open to the idea that he could teach us something valuable.

4. *The special ethical decision about whether or not to treat a client's sister*: Our final agenda item in this supervision session was quite rich because it involved discussing an ethical issue, using guided-discovery questioning to help Andrew think through the problem, employing a role-play to practice how he might diplomatically say "no" to the client's request, and advanced problem-solving to help decide how to manage confidentiality if Andrew opted to say "yes" to providing therapy to his client's sister. I noted that by asking Andrew to treat her sister, the client was giving him a vote of confidence and that he could feel good about this. At the same time, Andrew was uncomfortable about potentially being in a confidentiality bind if he treated both sisters, particularly if either one had clinically significant issues involving the other. I agreed that this could be a problem, but I wanted Andrew to think

things through more carefully rather than just avoiding what he found uncomfortable. Yes, a therapist's feelings of discomfort in response to a client's request can be an important cue that the request is professionally ill-advised. On the other hand, it could just be a case of Andrew's giving up too quickly and avoiding trying to solve the problem! Thus, I asked him if he could play devil's advocate and argue in favor of seeing the sister. Under what conditions might this be doable? In talking about this, we hit upon the concept of *availability* of treatment. Did the client's sister have other treatment options? Would she avail herself of any other therapists? We also noted that Andrew could talk explicitly with his client about confidentiality—for example, that he could treat the sister only if both clients agreed that confidentiality would be maintained *within the dyad* but that Andrew would be free to use his clinical judgment to share things with one client about the other. We did a role-play so that Andrew could practice nicely saying "no" to his client while giving her a solid rationale. This led to some problem solving, in which we came upon the idea that Andrew could talk to the sister by phone, thus making personal contact and perhaps encouraging her to get the help she needed, but he would give her a referral and try to boost her confidence in following through. I was happy that Andrew brought up this topic in supervision given that it is an ethical gray zone and thus requires some serious thought and advance troubleshooting before definitive action is taken with the client(s).

As we can see, this CBS meeting included points of focus that were not solely the province of CBT per se. Good mental health care supervision, regardless of the treatment modality, often helps supervisees to bolster their foundational competencies, such as cross-cultural responsiveness and ethical decision making. This well-structured supervision session was identifiable as CBT by virtue of its use of the conceptual language and techniques of this theoretical orientation, including the use of the CTRS as a way to rate Andrew's recorded session with G, with support and guidance offered in a congenial tone.

4

Handling Special Supervisory Issues

In this chapter we address issues and situations in supervision that are not the customary, routine aspects of training and clinical oversight that first come to mind when we think of clinical supervision. However, an important part of competency in supervision involves managing problems with supervisees, demonstrating a working knowledge of cross-cultural issues (Falender, Shafranske, & Falicov, 2014), having a strong foundation in clinical ethics (Pope & Vasquez, 2011; Thomas, 2014), and being willing and able to step up and deal with difficult clinical situations so that trainees get the extra help they need and clients are assured a reasonable standard of care. The following pages provide some guidance to cognitive–behavioral therapy (CBT) supervisors called upon to apply such knowledge and handle a sample of problematic scenarios.

http://dx.doi.org/10.1037/14950-005
Supervision Essentials for Cognitive–Behavioral Therapy, by C. F. Newman and D. A. Kaplan
Copyright © 2016 by the American Psychological Association. All rights reserved.

DEALING WITH SUPERVISEES WHO POSE CHALLENGES (ANXIETY, SHAME, DEFENSIVENESS)

For many supervisors, the time they spend with their supervisees is a uniquely rewarding part of their professional experience. However, it is inevitable that some supervisory relationships will be more challenging than others. Although each supervisor–supervisee dyad is unique, there are some common issues that may arise in the course of cognitive–behavioral supervision (CBS) that add a layer of difficulty to the experience.

Anxiety/Shame

Perhaps the most common area of difficulty in the supervisory relationship is trainee anxiety. Particularly for supervisees in the early stages of their training or those who have been trained in other modalities but are new to CBT, some anxiety is to be expected. Novice supervisees are in the position of having their fledgling CBT skills observed by a supervisor who may also be providing evaluative feedback to their home program, might later serve as a reference for a predoctoral internship or job, and ultimately have a say in whether they proceed through their training to become a licensed member of the profession. Under these circumstances, it would be surprising if trainees did not experience some anxiety in supervision. However, there are times when a supervisee's level of anxiety is high enough to interfere with the supervisory process and the supervisee's professional development. A highly anxious supervisee may have difficulty articulating the contents of a session with a client, identifying productive next steps in the therapeutic process, or encoding and utilizing supervisory feedback.

The CBT supervisor can do a good deal to mitigate supervisees' anxiety, beginning in the early phases of supervision. Supervisors would do well to communicate to their trainees early in supervision that mistakes are an expected part of the learning process and corrective feedback is routine. It is important for the CBT supervisor to make sure that suggestions for change are combined with feedback on things the supervisee has done well or areas in which he or she has shown growth. Just as it is unhelpful to point out and challenge every automatic thought a client mentions in session, overloading a supervisee only with feedback on areas for change can be bewildering or even demoralizing.

Supervisors can help to reduce their trainees' anxiety through modeling openness in supervision: for example, through judicious self-disclosure of the supervisor's imperfections as a therapist. Much as a therapist's brief, well-timed reflection on challenges that he or she has overcome can help normalize clients' experience of struggle or imperfection, the CBT supervisor can reference his or her own challenges as a beginning (or seasoned!) therapist to help supervisees feel more comfortable with their own learning curve. Supporting this approach is a study by Nelson, Barnes, Evans, and Triggiano (2008), which described how experienced, "wise" supervisors in their sample normalized difficulties as part of professional learning and development. In addition, such supervisors also used a modicum of humor in their humble self-disclosures of the foibles of their own work, as is seen in the following supervisor comment.

Supervisor: The first time I did progressive muscle relaxation intervention with a client, I was so nervous I think I probably made her *more* tense than before we started. To make matters worse, I started to have the hiccups! It was really a comedy of errors, I must admit. Later, I had to practice the technique a bunch of times outside of session before I really felt ready to use it with clients. I wonder if the same thing is happening when you try to use the exposure narrative that we talked about in here. Would it help if we practiced this some more, here in supervision?

Similarly, the supervisor can help decrease a supervisee's anxiety about "not knowing" by seeking consultation when appropriate. The following supervisor's comment is illustrative:

Supervisor: You know, I have some ideas about how to help your client through this impasse, but the things we've been talking about haven't been working as well as either of us would like. I know that Dr. E. just dealt with something very similar with one of her clients. Let's run this by her and see if she has any thoughts to share with us.

A suggestion such as this can serve as a useful reminder to supervisees at all levels of training that it is appropriate to consult with others when help is needed.

At times, supervisees' cognitions about the supervisory process itself or their own skill set might fuel the anxiety they experience in supervision. Thoughts and assumptions such as, "I have to act like I know what I'm doing, even when I don't" or "I should know how to do all this by now" might diminish supervisees' comfort in asking for help or admitting to gaps in knowledge. The CBT supervisor can, when appropriate, encourage a conversation about the supervisory process or the supervisee's self-evaluative thoughts. CBT techniques may be used to assess such cognitions and perhaps modify them in ways that facilitate the trainee's ability to participate more constructively in the supervisory process. The supervisor can steer clear of the pitfall of turning such an approach into *therapy* for the supervisee by staying squarely focused on the supervisee's anxiety and related thoughts about the *work* he or she is doing, as follows.

Supervisor: I've found that a lot of the techniques that are helpful for my clients—such as asking guided discovery questions in order to respond rationally to automatic thoughts—are also helpful for me when I'm having doubts about my work. It's also a great way for me to practice the techniques themselves. Would you be okay with our trying that for you right now? For example, I noticed that you sighed and looked a little disconcerted when I asked you how things went when you reviewed Mr. W.'s case conceptualization with him. What went through your mind just now?

Trainee: Well, I was thinking that he didn't agree with some of the things we talked about in here. I didn't know how to respond to that or where to go from there.

Supervisor: Thanks for telling me. That's important to know. Here's a typical guided discovery question you can ask yourself. "What did it mean to you" that he disagreed?

Trainee: Well, I guess that I got it wrong. And that you would probably be really disappointed in me because we spent so much time on it in here—like maybe if I had explained it better it would have gone over better.

Supervisor: Thanks for sharing that with me. I wonder if we can take a few minutes and look at some other possibilities for what might have happened with Mr. W, and also try to look at this situation in a way *other* than that you're doing something wrong or risking disappointing me. Is that OK with you?

Trainee: That would be a big help, actually.

Supervisor: OK, great. So one possibility is that I might have been disappointed in you. Any other ones?

Trainee: Well, you might have been wondering what you got wrong, too.

Supervisor: Absolutely. We did work on this together. I could just as easily think that I disappointed you! But I don't know that "getting it wrong" is necessarily a bad thing. Sometimes we can get as much information out of what doesn't go well with a client as we can out of what does go well. Maybe we can spend some time thinking about what we can learn from Mr. Ws reactions. Based on that idea, what's another rational response we can apply here?

Trainee: Maybe we can actually improve the case conceptualization, based on Mr. W.'s comments, or maybe incorporate his reactions into our conceptualization of his response style when someone tries to give him well-meaning feedback.

Supervisor: Exactly. That would be very constructive. Notice how you can rationally respond to this situation without having to feel badly about it. Learning doesn't always have to be painful!

Although the technique illustrated does not differ substantially from that which might be used in therapy, the aim is to explore the trainee's thoughts as they relate to his or her work at present and does not necessitate delving into the trainee's personal history or relationships with others. This highly circumscribed use of the technique maintains the important boundary between teaching and treating. When supervisees spontaneously stray into the area of revealing too much about themselves (as they may do in their personal therapy), the supervisor has to find a nonshaming way of asking them to refrain from doing so. The following supervisor sample comment provides an illustration.

Supervisor: I appreciate your trust in me, but it's not necessary for you to disclose so much about your personal life and challenges in supervision. I want to be understanding about any stressors that might be affecting you in your work here, but I also want to draw a line between supervision and therapy. That way we'll keep our supervisory relationship in the proper zone, and frankly, it's better for you if we do that. I hope that doesn't sound dismissive or uncaring in any way. It definitely matters to me how you feel and how positive your experience in supervision is.

Resistance/Defensiveness

Supervisees' anxiety may at times present as defensiveness or resistance to incorporating the supervisor's suggestions on how to proceed in treatment. The simple cognitive restructuring technique discussed in the previous section for addressing anxiety also sometimes proves useful when a trainee appears resistant to supervision. However, there are times when supervisees' resistance to feedback involves something more than anxiety. Not all trainees seek supervision in CBT voluntarily. Some may engage in CBT training and supervision as a requirement of their program but have a strong preference for another model of case conceptualization and intervention. In such cases, a supervisee may be reluctant to employ CBT techniques suggested by the supervisor or believe that being asked to do so is an unwelcome challenge to his or her own preferred way of thinking.

An apparently resistant supervisee may also have misconceptions about CBT. Consider, for example, the following interaction between one of the authors (DK) and an advanced psychiatry resident who had been trained primarily in psychodynamic psychotherapies.

Supervisor: It sounds like the client was really in a lot of pain when she was talking about her mother's leaving her at home alone for the weekend when she was a teenager.

Trainee: Yes, she was crying until she had a hard time catching her breath. She was very distressed. At that point, it just seemed cruel to do what you were asking me to do—to ask about her thinking while she was in so much pain.

Supervisor: Let's imagine for the moment that this weren't your "CBT client." What might you have done if you were working with her in a different modality?

Trainee: Well, I would have empathized with her.

Supervisor: Absolutely. Empathy and validation are very appropriate and helpful in that moment. Were you thinking that a CBT approach would instruct you *not* to do this?

Trainee: Well, you keep telling me that we're supposed to be evaluating her *thoughts*.

Supervisor: In the right context, with the right tone, that's true, but I can tell you straight out that in CBT it would be extremely important for you to provide the client with empathy at such a moment. We could role-play that situation if you wish. You could be the client, and I can illustrate how a CBT clinician might respond, perhaps trying to understand the client's thinking in the process, but always with warmth, support, and caring.

Note in the example how the supervisor does not bristle at the supervisee's suggestion that assessing a vulnerable client's thoughts would be "cruel" but rather takes an approach that is more exploratory and instructive. The supervisor recognizes that the supervisee maintains a faulty belief about CBT itself, and the supervisor is in a position to modify this belief, in a nondefensive, noncruel way! The supervisor remains collaborative with this therapist-in-training, looking for common ground, and not getting into a power struggle (see Sudak et al., 2015).

In their overview of CBS, Liese and Beck (1997) discuss some of the common misconceptions about CBT that might interfere with a productive supervisory relationship. Among them are the beliefs that CBT is unconcerned with the role of the client's historical, developmental experiences; that CBT views the therapeutic relationship as being relatively unimportant; and that those who practice CBT are unconcerned with the client's emotions, choosing instead to focus exclusively on the client's "distorted" thinking. A supervisee who has been exposed only to the myths or stereotypes of CBT might well be resistant to attempting to treat a client from a cognitive–behavioral perspective. Thus, it is important for a supervisor who is experiencing his or her supervisee as resistant to explore the degree to which the supervisee maintains some of these inaccurate viewpoints of CBT.

It is important to distinguish between a supervisee who is resistant to working with clients within a CBT framework and one who is resistant to being supervised in general, the latter of which may indicate a more serious problem. Periodic consultation among supervisors who are working with the same supervisee or, when relevant, consulting with a supervisee's training program can be helpful in allowing the CBT supervisor to contextualize defensiveness and resistance and identify appropriate strategies for addressing them. When possible, these strategies should be discussed with the supervisee in a way that clearly lays out the nature of the problem and specifies targets for change. The following are examples of ways that supervisors might identify and operationalize problems that might arise in working with resistant supervisees:

> "I'm required to cosign your notes, but you haven't been bringing the charts to our meetings. Can we talk about what's getting in the way and come up with a plan to remedy this?"

> "We have been talking for a few weeks now about working with your client to develop strategies for coping with her intense anger. I notice that you have spent a lot of time talking with her about the historical origins of her anger but not as much time discussing her current behavior when she gets angry. This concerns me because I haven't heard that there's been much change in her behavior, and she is on probation at work due to her anger outbursts there. Let's talk about how you're viewing the problem and what you think about the problem-solving interventions I've been suggesting."

> "I'm hoping we can talk a little bit today about our interactions in supervision. I've noticed that we have disagreed quite frequently on numerous clinical and operational issues. I would like for us to find a way to become more collaborative because the clients' well-being and your training goals are better served if we can find points of agreement."

"I wanted to let you know that in our quarterly supervisors meeting it came up that none of your supervisors has ever received a recorded session from you. This is one of the requirements of the training program, so we need to find a way to solve this problem. What are your views on this matter?"

These comments represent an approach that is appropriately assertive—after all, the supervisors are in a position of authority, and they need to exercise that authority when necessary—while also expressing hopefulness about coming to a positive resolution. The overarching message from the supervisor is, "We have a specific problem we need to deal with as a team. Here is the problem as I see it. I also welcome your views about the problem. Let us promptly find a collaborative way to solve the problem, for the clients' benefit, and yours." The supervisees' response to this entreaty is informative. If supervisees seize the opportunity to try to improve their clinical work and interactions with the supervisor, it provides evidence of their commitment to learning, capacity for good communication and problem-solving skills, and prioritization of constructive conflict resolution over doubling down on the problematic status quo. On the other hand, if they respond unfavorably and with negative affect, this may provide evidence of a more serious issue that may need to be addressed at the institutional level. If the supervisor approaches the problem in a composed, thoughtful, hopeful, and constructive way, the supervisee's response will provide useful information that is mostly reflective of *the supervisee's* attitudes and affect.

The Supervisor's "Contribution" to the Problem

At times, a supervisor's own assumptions, attitudes, and behaviors might impede the supervisory process and increase trainees' anxiety, defensiveness, or resistance to supervision. For example, a supervisor who focuses exclusively on supervisees' areas that need to be improved and consistently fails to highlight their strengths and successes might leave his or her supervisees with the impression that they can do nothing right. Similarly, a supervisor who presumes that he or she is the sole expert and that his or her supervisees have nothing to contribute to the supervisory dialogue may find that supervision comes to resemble a monologue in which the supervisor is lecturing to an increasingly frustrated supervisee. Supervisors who recognize, validate, and incorporate the unique skill sets that their supervisees bring to the table, some of which may differ from the supervisor's own, may find that their supervisees are more receptive to learning from the supervisor's way of thinking and areas of expertise. This may be particularly true for CBT supervisors who are working with supervisees who are new to CBT but have been trained extensively in other modalities and theoretical orientations. A supervisor who fails to recognize and acknowledge the skills that his or her supervisee has already developed loses an opportunity for a productive and collaborative exchange of ideas and for the supervisor's own learning.

In light of the role that supervisors' own behaviors can play in their supervisees' openness or resistance to supervision, it is important for feedback about supervision to be bidirectional. The more readily a supervisee can share information about what is helpful and not helpful in the supervisor's approach to supervision, the more fruitful the supervisory relationship can become. Given the inherent power imbalance in the supervisory relationship, feedback from the supervisee is more likely to be obtained when the supervisor asks for it proactively. This helps to create an environment in which the supervisee's observations and requests for change are met with acceptance and nondefensiveness. Metasupervision, to be discussed in Chapter 5, may be a useful aid to supervisors in examining their own role in the ups and downs of the supervisory relationship.

It is extremely important for supervisors to exhibit a high level of motivation to resolve any strains in their working relationship with supervisees in a positive way. In the same way that a therapist's successfully resolving an alliance strain with a client can result in significant therapeutic gains (Strauss et al., 2006), a supervisor's interpersonally adept handling of tension with a supervisee can present the latter with an excellent model for conflict resolution (Safran & Muran, 2001). The supervisee can then bring that same skill and spirit to his or her work with clients. For a supervisor to achieve the goal of reaching a positive accord with a supervisee after a disagreement, the supervisor has to be self-aware, empathic, and mindful of the big picture (helping clients and clinical trainees), rather than being focused on winning an argument or asserting authority.

Part of being *self-aware* is being willing to be a healthy skeptic of one's own thoughts and to reflect on one's own emotions without simply acting on them. In supervision, this means the supervisor is willing to reassess his or her own ideas about how to properly manage the supervisees' training and the clients' care. As an example of this process, many years ago one of us (CN) supervised a visiting professor who was spending her sabbatical getting more clinical training in CBT. Given that her license to practice psychology was in a different state, she required full-fledged supervision (i.e., not just consultation) from a practitioner licensed in Pennsylvania (the home state of the Center for Cognitive Therapy). Our working relationship proceeded smoothly until we disagreed about the treatment of a young man who had an anxiety disorder manifested by clinically significant avoidance. I watched a video of one of the supervisee's sessions with this client and noticed that although she was very empathic toward the client (and it was clear that the therapeutic relationship was strong), the client easily was able to talk his way out of doing any exposure exercises and behavioral experiments. In the supervision session, I expressed my concern, saying that the supervisee needed to be more directive; otherwise, the client would simply use therapy for emotional support and nothing more. I suggested that she give him explicit feedback about his avoidance patterns. In response, the supervisee called my attention to the case conceptualization, highlighting a learning history in which the client's father used to routinely deride him for his failings, making demands for change that served mainly to poison their relationship and undermine the client's self-confidence. She stated that she did not want to risk replicating that sort of relationship, which she feared she would do if she were to lower her degree of unconditional acceptance and increase the level of confrontation in session. She added that she did not want to reinforce the client's "incompetency" schema and associated shame by pointing out his failure to participate in exposure exercises and behavioral experiments.

At first, my supervisee and I had difficulty hearing each other as we continued to make our own points, and we progressively became more frustrated. At last, I made a process comment on our difference of opinion and wondered aloud if we could find a middle ground on which we could agree and build a foundation for ongoing interventions for the client. I took the lead, saying that I was going to take stock of my staunch "anti-avoidance" position and try to moderate it. I invited the supervisee to do the same with regard to her "unconditional acceptance" model. I acknowledged that I felt frustrated when I watched the video, thinking that the client was "taking the path of least resistance" in treatment, that the supervisee was positively reinforcing this, and consequently the client was not getting an adequate "dose" of CBT.

However, I acknowledged that I did not always feel optimally empathic toward certain avoidant clients, and I recalled aloud that some years earlier my own CBT supervisor observed that my male clients with anxiety disorders tended to leave treatment prematurely, whereas my female clients with anxiety disorders stayed and did well. Upon further reflection, I had to admit that I was "tougher" on my male clients than my female clients, a bit of implicit sexism that I was not proud to reveal. My supervisor had hypothesized that I was calmer and more understanding of the women clients' feelings of stress but more apt to be "an aggressive sports coach" with the male clients (as if to say, "Get back on that field and show what you're made of!"). I worked on this problem over the years, including examining my personal history of being uncompassionate and intolerant of my own anxiety, but perhaps I still had more work to do!

In the here and now of my supervision session, I stated that there was evidence from my previous clinical work that I needed to be a little more understanding (and less demanding) of male clients with anxiety. Following my cue, my supervisee told me about her tendency to be an all-doing "caretaker" of vulnerable people in her life, and how she could probably benefit from expanding her repertoire so as to ask more of others, including her clients, not to mention certain people in her life.

At first glance, this vignette may seem like an example of turning supervision into therapy, but the fact that the process was *shared*, with supervisor and supervisee equally partaking in a process of self-evaluation to help a client, meant that the boundary into treatment was not crossed. This is better understood as an example of interpersonal process in CBS (Safran & Muran, 2001), in which I needed to find a balance between seeing (and acknowledging) the merits of what the supervisee was doing and assertively and directly asking her to do more. As Milne and Reiser (2014) noted, "managing this tension between support and challenge is at the core of effective supervision" (p. 412). In our mutual exercise of self-reflection, my supervisee and I felt more at ease with each other, understood each other's position a little better, and came to the revolutionary conclusion that it was possible to be empathic toward a client *and* be more assertive in promoting difficult but powerful evidence-based interventions! Empathy and directiveness are not mutually exclusive therapeutic activities in CBT! Who knew?

TRAINEE IMPAIRMENT/SKILL DEFICIT (REMEDIATION AND GATEKEEPING)

The close working relationship between supervisor and trainee may at times result in the trainee's spontaneous disclosure of his or her current challenges in life. For example, supervisors may become aware of trainees' difficulty adjusting to a training site or a new geographic location, personal or familial illness, relationship breakups, and trainees' own struggles with depression, anxiety, or conditions that may mirror those of the clients they treat. Concerned as the supervisor might be about his or her trainee's personal well-being in such circumstances, it is important to ascertain if challenges such as those mentioned affect a trainee's ability to meet expected levels of performance. When a trainee's difficulties clearly affect his or her ability to conduct therapy safely, ethically, and with an appropriate level of skill, a trainee may be considered impaired. *Impairment* has been formally defined as, "A condition that interferes with professional functioning to the extent it negatively impacts clients/patients or makes effective service delivery impossible" (Kaslow et al., 2007, p. 481). It should be noted that the concept of impairment as it applies to the safe practice of therapy does not refer to the presence of physical or mental disabilities requiring a modification in *nonessential* job functions as mandated by the Americans With Disabilities Act (DeLeire, 2000). Neither does it refer to transient, contextual factors affecting a therapist's work, such as in the case of a supervisee who is not at his or her best as a result of going through a process of grieving a loss.

It is when dealing with an impaired supervisee that the supervisor's tripartite role as overseer of client safety, facilitator of the supervisee's professional development, and gatekeeper to the profession comes to the fore. The supervisor working with an impaired trainee must be mindful of all aspects of this role simultaneously and work to address each one appropriately.

Client Safety

The well-being of clients being treated by a trainee for whom questions of impairment have arisen requires significant attention and scaffolding on the part of the supervisor. A possible starting point in determining whether the difficulties the trainee is experiencing rise to the level of impairment—or conversely, can improve with additional assistance—is more frequent supervision and more direct observation of the supervisee's work, such as via videotaped sessions. Supervisors might also be called upon to sit in on sessions with the supervisee and the client or conduct an independent assessment to evaluate clients' safety. In cases in which it is determined that the supervisee is unable to continue to treat a particular client, the supervisor facilitates the transfer of the client's care in as smooth and undisruptive a manner as possible. This may include having the supervisor directly assume responsibility for treating the client until the supervisee is able to resume work or until another supervisee can take over for the duration of treatment.

Supervisee Development

Although supervisee impairment generally is thought of as being distinct from the supervisee's having skills deficits, there may be times when these two factors interact. For example, a supervisee who is actively struggling with panic disorder may be less willing or able to facilitate an interoceptive exposure exercise with a client who has a similar problem. Although the CBT supervisor is not (and does not function as) the supervisee's therapist, there are instances in which clinical supervision can help to address the issues interfering with the trainee's professional functioning, as illustrated here.

Supervisor: I'm noticing that although we've discussed using overbreathing exercises with Ms. X to address her panic symptoms, you seem worried about trying it out in session. Can you tell me a little bit about what you imagine might happen if you tried it?

Trainee: Well, I know that feeling where your heart starts pounding and you can't catch your breath, and it's really awful. I just don't want to put anyone else through that for no reason.

Supervisor: It's true that the sensation you describe can feel really frightening at first. If I hear you right, it sounds like you think that if you try some of these strategies with Ms. X, it will just result in her feeling really awful, and nothing good will come of it. Does that sound right?

Trainee: Well, when you put it that way, it sounds a little extreme. I know that interoceptive exposures can be very helpful in the long run. But in the short term, it's really hard on the client, and the therapist has to be super confident in order to make this work, and frankly I'm not sure I'm super confident. So I guess I'm looking for alternative ways to help this client and to bypass the exposures if possible.

Supervisor: I appreciate your candor about how you feel, and I'm glad that at some level you can make an objective evaluation about the efficacy of exposure exercises so that you don't view them as being unhelpful. Even though you're not very confident right now, are you open to the possibility that with some graded practice of your own—maybe in some role-playing in supervision—that you can gradually *gain* some confidence so that you will be able to implement interoceptive exposure exercises into your work with clients who have panic disorder?

Trainee: (*Hesitant*). I would like to say yes. What would the graded practice look like?

The supervisor could then use supervision time to review the rationale and the expected outcome for interoceptive exposure and to role-play as a client so that the supervisee can practice an intervention such as overbreathing without fear of making a real client "feel worse." This sort of role-playing can be done multiple times, with the supervisor enacting different challenges, such as a client who stops taking part or who reacts with distress. The supervisee will then have the opportunity to practice reparative interventions in a safe environment and see that even a less-than-ideal outcome at the moment of the intervention may still have psychoeducational and therapeutic effects on a client if it is processed properly and empathically. If the supervisee benefits from the supervisory role-play, the supervisor can then raise the bar and ask if the supervisee is willing to take the role of the client who will be doing the interoceptive exposure. If the supervisee agrees, the supervisor will be able to model how to effectively and sensitively handle a client who has misgivings about a procedure. If the supervisee declines to do the exercise in the role of the client, the supervisor does not then press the matter or otherwise risk turning the interaction into something akin to doing therapy with the supervisee. Rather, the supervisor can suggest that the supervisee continue to practice the procedure as a therapist but also consider seeking outside therapeutic help to learn to decatastrophize the physical sensations of anxiety and panic. The following is a sample comment from a supervisor in such a situation. Note the hopeful, helpful tone used to motivate (rather than risk shaming) the supervisee.

Supervisor: I think you're in a position where you can continue to practice implementing the interoceptive exposure exercises so you can ultimately do them with an actual client. But I can promise you that if you practice the method on yourself—in other words, if you can do the overbreathing yourself, maybe in the presence of your own CBT therapist—you will benefit doubly. You will find that you can manage your own fight-or-flight symptoms better, which is important in its own right for your quality of life. But even more, you will feel that measure of "super confidence" that has been eluding you. I can tell you from my own experience as a therapist that when you deal with your own biggest issues, you feel so much better about asking your clients to deal with *their* biggest issues. You will feel that your therapeutic messages to yourself and your clients are *congruent*, and this is valuable. What do you think about that?

Gatekeeper Function

At times, concerns about the level of a supervisee's impairment may lead the supervisor to question the advisability of the supervisee's continuing his or her training. When clinical supervision takes place in the context of a private arrangement between the supervisor and supervisee, well-articulated guidelines for the termination of supervision ideally should be stated in the supervisory contract put in place at the beginning of supervision. The supervisor may also benefit from consulting with regional and national ethics committees and licensing boards to determine an appropriate course of action (Kaslow et al., 2007).

The ethical and legal issues involved in dealing with an impaired trainee become more complex when supervision is provided within an agency or institutional setting. In such cases, clinical supervisors should be certain to consult with their own administrative supervisors regarding any existing policies and procedures involved in the modification or termination of the supervisory relationship. This may also involve consulting with the organization's human resources or legal departments, particularly when taking any action that involves a trainee's suspension, mandating of mental health or substance abuse treatment, or terminating the supervisee from a training position. When a supervisee is a matriculated student at another training institution or from another discipline, the supervisor or an appropriate representative from the supervisor's adjunct training site should also be in contact with the supervisee's home institution or training program.

POWER AND EVALUATION

Inherent in all supervisory relationships, no matter how collaborative and no matter how much the supervisor may value an egalitarian teaching style, is an imbalance of power between supervisor and supervisee (see Murphy & Wright, 2005; Patel, 2004). Most supervisory relationships are between an unlicensed therapist and a supervisor who holds ultimate legal and ethical responsibility for the well-being of the clients under the supervisee's care (Campbell, 2005). In addition, the clinical supervisor often is responsible for supervisees' formal evaluations, thus influencing the latter's progression to higher levels of training and their eventual eligibility to enter into the profession fully credentialed. One way in which supervisors can empower their supervisees is by recommending resources that inform them about what to expect in supervision and how best to navigate the process (e.g., Falender & Shafranske, 2012, in press).

As noted, the attuned supervisor will bring up the question of evaluation proactively and early in supervision, stating that evaluative feedback is an integral and expected part of supervision. Supervisees ideally should be aware of the objective criteria on which they will be evaluated and, if a formal evaluation form will be used, given a template of the form at the start of supervision. Although training may take place in a setting that uses its own evaluation form, supervisees who are specifically interested in improving their CBT skills might also be given the option of having their progress assessed with a CBT-specific instrument, such as the CTRS (Young & Beck, 1980). It is fitting and proper for supervisors to communicate with their supervisees face to face about the formal, written evaluations. This process allows the supervisees to provide feedback about how their perceptions of their own progress compare with the supervisors' assessment and similarly allows supervisors to explain their rationales for their evaluations. When supervisors handle this process competently, and when supervisees are reasonably receptive, it can serve as a positive learning experience, and any unfortunate miscommunications or misunderstandings can be addressed and perhaps resolved in a mutually satisfactory way.

It is to be expected that supervisees will have areas of strength as well as areas for further growth and development, most of which can be addressed in the context of routine supervision meetings. However, at times the magnitude of a supervisee's skills deficit requires a more formal and concrete plan of remediation. As stated, when this is the case, it is important that the supervisor follow all policies and procedures developed by the institution under whose auspices he or she is supervising. Thus, a supervisor who is considering implementing a formal remediation plan for a supervisee should incorporate input from the supervisee's other immediate supervisors, his or her program or department chair, and the director of training at the site at which the supervisee is training.

All formal feedback concerning the need for remediation should be put in writing and discussed in terms of measurable and operationalizable outcomes and objectives (e.g., "Supervisee will complete charting within 48 hours of seeing a client"). For feedback to be educational rather than punitive, it should also include a plan for helping the supervisee address areas of weakness. This may include additional supervision sessions, providing the supervisee with suitably instructive readings, and/or helping the supervisee develop a plan for improving his or her time management skills. Finally, a remediation plan should include a specific date at which progress toward goals will be reevaluated and additional steps will be suggested—including, if necessary, termination from the practicum site or program—if deficits are not remediated.

AWARENESS OF AND SENSITIVITY TO MULTICULTURAL/DIVERSITY ISSUES

Supervisors play an important role in helping supervisees to appreciate the relevance of cultural issues in the application of CBT to diverse populations. Castro, Barrera, and Holleran Steiker (2010) noted that "culture consists of the worldviews and lifeways of a group of people . . . transmitted from elders to children, and [conferring] members . . . with a sense of peoplehood, unity, and belonging . . ." (p. 216). Culture is associated with such factors as language, food, social structure and customs, symbols and rituals, beliefs, and a striving for survival and continuation. The authors cite evidence that when clinicians adapt therapy to be more comprehensible to and respectful of a client who identifies strongly with a given culture, it improves the client's engagement in the process of treatment.

When a client is of a nonmainstream cultural group (i.e., outside the majority or plurality in a given societal milieu), it is particularly important for the supervisor to bring the potential importance of this topic to the supervisee's attention. Similarly, when the supervisee self-identifies as part of a nonmainstream cultural group, the supervisor needs to be sensitive to this and proactive in discussing the ways in which the supervisee's cultural identity affects his or her experience in his or her work as a clinician (see Iwamasa, Pai, & Sorocco, 2006). Self-knowledge is an important part of cultural competence. As an exercise, supervisors and supervisees alike can ask themselves the question, "Who am I as a cultural being?" (Falender & Shafranske, 2012), giving consideration to how their self-perceptions interact with their perceptions of the cultural characteristics of those for whom they are clinically responsible. Regardless of whether it is the supervisor, the supervisee, the client, or some combination of them who represent a minority population in society, it is incumbent upon the supervisor to be proactive in creating a positive atmosphere for discussing the role of culture in therapy and supervision. Supervisors and supervisees may have a great deal to learn from each other with regard to cultural issues and their effect on therapy and supervision, which not only benefits the clients but also helps supervisors to grow and supervisees to feel more positively about supervision (Ancis & Ladany, 2010; Inman, 2006).

One of the challenges in being culturally sensitive is being accurately empathic with clients whose life experiences as cultural minorities are dramatically different from those of the therapist and/or supervisor, and arguably "unknowable" (as in the case of Andrew and his supervisor trying to understand the racial discrimination experienced by the African-American client in Chapter 3). Rather than falling prey to "all or none" thinking, in which one feels helpless to understand the client at one extreme or insists that "I know *exactly* how the client feels" at the other extreme, there is a middle ground approach. This moderate tack involves actively trying to *imagine* what it must be like to be this particular client (similar to a "method actor" researching a role to *be* the character), while simultaneously acknowledging that this approach does not replicate the actual experience of the client. Supervisors can help their trainees practice this technique via the use of hypothetical questions, a method that is consistent with "guided discovery," one of the core features of a well-run CBT session (therapy or supervision). For example, supervisors can ask their supervisees, "How would you feel if you were . . .

- a sexual minority who has never 'come out' to his family and feels all alone?
- someone struggling to speak English as a second language and often dealing with being derided by people who speak only English?
- new to this country, but you had close family members 'stuck' elsewhere in the world?
- a young person who is acculturated here but living with parents who are 'old country' in their lifestyle and attitudes, so you were torn between two worlds?
- judged by others at first glance all your life (e.g., because your skin was a different color or because you were permanently in a wheelchair)?"

Entertaining such hypothetical questions in supervision often stimulates meaningful conversations that can help trainees increase their culturally related empathic capacity. This is a good starting point in fostering "cultural humility" (Falender & Shafranske, 2012). Another important step is conceptualizing clients' behaviors in light of their cultural background and adapting one's clinical responses accordingly. For example, in the following sample transcript, the supervisor and supervisee talk about the potential significance of the client's repeated, deliberate skipping of a self-report inventory item. The client is a never-married, devoutly religious woman of color who was born and raised in Africa.

Trainee: I have been keeping track of the client's Beck Depression Inventory (BDI-II) scores, and the client has been very consistent in filling out the form before every session. But I should tell you that there is one item that she always skips, which is the one that asks about any diminishing of sexual interest. Should I ask her to fill that one out? Should I just let it go?

Supervisor: That's a good question. Usually, I would just advise you to ask her in a sensitive way about her reasons for skipping that item. Ordinarily, I would think that maybe we're talking about a client's run-of-the-mill embarrassment about answering a question about sex.

Trainee: Or maybe there could be a history of sexual trauma that makes her choose to avoid anything that reminds her about sex. You know, she also gave sparse answers at intake when she was asked about posttraumatic stress symptoms.

Supervisor: And that would be a very good reason *not* to ignore her omission of the item that asks about sex because it could be a highly clinically relevant topic that might never get addressed if we passively allow her to avoid the issue. On the other hand, we want to be respectful of the client's boundaries, and this may be one way in which she is setting a boundary—by skipping the question. And then there's the matter of her cultural background to consider.

Trainee: I was thinking about that. Maybe as a single woman who strongly identifies with her cultural origins, she is supposed to think that sex is irrelevant for her, and perhaps it would be an affront if I asked her to give consideration to questions about her libido, even though that's relevant to clients with depression like her and relevant to most of the clients I work with.

Supervisor: I wonder who we can consult on this matter. Maybe we can put out a message on the listserv of the Association for Behavioral and Cognitive Therapy and discreetly ask for a confidential back-channel consultation from a clinician who has had firsthand experience with this client's cultural background.

Trainee: I'm relieved to hear this. I thought I was doing something wrong by not collecting the BDI-II data properly, but I was very hesitant to bring up this topic with this particular client, knowing her cultural origins and identity.

Supervisor: Not to worry. You did exactly the right thing. The client's well-being always comes first. Data collection is important but not as important as respecting the client's boundaries, and clients like this one may have stricter boundaries than others. Still, on the chance that she has a history of sexual trauma, we don't want to avoid the topic of sex entirely without first consulting on the matter and maybe thinking of other ways that we can approach the issue of past trauma. For now, until we can get more information, continue to allow her to skip the last question on the BDI-II. But please keep your antennae up for any comments your client may make that signal that she has something to say either about sex or trauma, or both. That would be the time to be quiet and let her talk while you listen intently and maybe only give her some gentle guidance.

As Castro et al. (2010) point out, the effort to incorporate multicultural perspectives into empirically supported treatments represents a balance between nomothetic formulations of diagnoses and distress that emphasize treatment fidelity and idiographic understandings of a client's presentation that call for individualization and flexibility. The evidence that cultural adaptations result in better treatment outcomes for ethnic minority clients is mixed and inconsistent (e.g., Griner & Smith, 2006; Huey & Polo, 2008) and may depend in part on the specific cultural group for which the intervention is adapted, the degree to which core concepts of the original evidence-based treatment are preserved in the modified format, and the degree of acculturation of the client population.

There are many non-CBT–specific resources that may be of help to the culturally attuned supervisor. For example, the American Psychological Association and Commission on Accreditation (2009), in collaboration with the Council of National Psychological Associations for the Advancement of Ethnic Minority Interests (2009), generated a series of culture-specific recommendations for psychology education and training. Along the same lines, there are informative readings outside the field of mental health care per se that can be extraordinarily elucidating regarding the difficulties involved in balancing professional protocol with cultural beliefs and rituals. An excellent example is the nonfiction book *The Spirit Catches You and You Fall Down* (Fadiman, 1997). This book chronicles the painful and ultimately tragic story of a young refugee girl's odyssey through an American medical establishment that struggled to understand the girl's serious neurological symptoms in their own right, much less through the lens of her Hmong culture. This volume provides no simple answers to a complex matter; it does not point fingers of blame toward medical personnel or the girl's family but rather enlightens the reader regarding the many ways that vital communication and understanding between practitioners and clients/patients (and their families) can be derailed owing to a clash of cultures. CBT supervisors who read this book will be enriched, and if they choose to assign this text to supervisees (and/or students in a supervision course), the result will be meaningful discussions that will improve the supervisees' cultural competency.

AWARENESS OF AND RESPONSIVENESS TO LEGAL/ETHICAL ISSUES

A comprehensive discussion of the myriad specific ethical and legal issues that may arise in the course of clinical or supervisory work is beyond the scope of this book (for a comprehensive summary of some of the more common of these issues see Koocher, Shafranske, & Falender, 2008). However, some central features of ethical supervision warrant mention and description here. The supervisory relationship itself provides an opportunity for the supervisor to model the ethical principles at the core of the profession. Through weekly interactions with the supervisee, the supervisor demonstrates adherence to key principles such as beneficence, integrity, justice, and respect for all persons (American Psychological Association, 2002, 2010). The ethical clinical supervisor also avoids any actions within the supervisory relationship that violate the ethics code, such as exploitative dual relationships.

The ethically adept supervisor is aware of the more subtle ways in which ethical issues may arise in supervision. For example, the supervisor recognizes when the clinical material a supervisee presents falls outside of the supervisor's area of competence and models ethical conduct by consulting with colleagues and/or additional educational materials. More broadly, when supervisors are struggling with life crises or other serious problems, they must wisely self-monitor (and/or seek peer consultation) to ensure that their personal issues do not interfere with their ability to provide adequate, unbiased, and effective supervision. Pursuant to this matter, supervisors need to be prepared to make arrangements for both appropriate self-care and adequate supervision coverage for their trainees to ensure the quality of the supervisees' training experience and the appropriate monitoring of the clients under their care.

Clinical supervisors would do well to be aware of any legal statutes relevant to the clients under their supervision and make their supervisees aware of them as well. For example, in the United States, supervisors make it a point to familiarize themselves with the guidelines for reporting child or elder abuse or neglect in their states and discuss these in detail with their supervisees early in supervision and again when such matters become clinically relevant.

Perhaps the legal principle most relevant to clinical supervision is that of *respondeat superior*—literally, "let the master answer." The term refers to the principle that employers—or, in this case, clinical supervisors—are legally responsible for the conduct of employees under their supervision. Given the additional possibility that clients may pose a danger to themselves or others, it is important for supervisors to be aware of the ways in which this doctrine informs their supervisory responsibility. On a basic administrative level, supervisors are prepared to endorse the contents of any therapy notes they countersign. Clinically, it means that supervisors attest to the fact that the treatment that they are overseeing is one they believe to be relevant, appropriately delivered, and reflective of the best interests of the client.

Although some legal and ethical issues may be clear-cut (e.g., obtaining a signed release before using a video of a client for educational training), there inevitably will be times when supervisees bring up ethical gray areas (as described in Chapter 3). The ideal supervisory climate for managing such matters is one in which active discussion of ethical and legal issues is woven throughout supervision. The supervisor should be proactive in highlighting these ethical gray areas as they arise and make space for trainees to engage in reflection about how best to address them. This involves differentiating areas of ambiguity from areas that are frankly nonnegotiable under the laws and ethics code under which the supervisee operates.

The following clinical dilemma arose in the course of a supervisee's work with a client who was highly ambivalent about continuing in therapy and whose core schema was *mistrust*, especially regarding authority figures. Note how the supervisor helps guide a discussion of the relevant ethical considerations.

Trainee: Something happened this week in a session with a client that has really bothered me. Ms. X asked me to write a letter for her verifying that she uses her dog as an emotional support animal and that she should be allowed to take him on the plane with her when she goes to visit her mother. I know she loves this dog, and it's going to be a really stressful trip for her, given the complicated relationship she has with her mother. But she's asking me to write a letter saying that the dog serves a formal therapeutic purpose, and I think that's stretching the truth. On the other hand, we have spent so much time talking about whether she can trust me. I'm worried that if I give her a flat-out "no," it will damage our therapeutic relationship. I wound up telling her that I needed to consult with my supervisor about this because I didn't know what to say.

Supervisor: I understand why this situation causes you some consternation. Requests like this one are hard to respond to when you're put on the spot, especially when dealing with a client with trust issues. I'm glad that you were able to communicate to the client that you couldn't give her a firm answer until you had the chance to think about it and talk it over in supervision. Deferring an answer so that you can consult first is often an appropriate strategy.

Trainee: Is there a hard-and-fast rule or policy about these sorts of letters?

Supervisor: I don't believe there is anything specific in the ethics code about writing letters on behalf of clients per se, but I think we can look at some general ethical principles for guidance. There are a few issues at play here—let's go through them and see if things become clearer.

Trainee: I really want her to see me as someone she can trust and who has her best interests at heart. At the same time, I don't want her to get the idea that she is entitled to whatever she wants and that I'm her unconditional advocate. She needs some gentle limit-setting, too.

Supervisor: Thinking conceptually in terms of schemas, you don't want to reinforce her *mistrust* schema by saying "no," but you also don't want to reinforce her *entitlement* schema by just saying "Yes, whatever you want." Let's see what we can derive from the ethical guidelines as well. [*Pausing* *to reflect*] It would seem that we have to consider the ethical principles of *beneficence and nonmaleficence, fidelity and responsibility*, and *integrity*. In other words, you want to help your client within reasonable limits, earn her trust, and not cause her any harm. On the other hand, you want to be truthful—in this case, it means not writing a letter you think misrepresents the facts, especially if it creates negative consequence for others and for society. What are your thoughts on that?

Trainee: Well, it's not as though my client taking her dog on the flight is going to harm anybody else, at least I don't think so. I know these things are done and that airlines supposedly have guidelines and safeguards. I just don't want to send the wrong message that I will automatically sign on to whatever my client wants, even if my viewpoint differs somewhat.

Supervisor: Okay, is there a way to support her *without* giving this message of entitlement and without being untruthful?

Trainee: I guess I could write a letter on her behalf but be very careful to stick to the facts. I could truthfully state that she is in therapy, that she has official diagnoses of major depression and panic disorder, that she is making a stressful trip, that she lives alone except for her one companion—which is her dog—and that she would benefit from the companionship of her pet. But I'm not saying that she *has* to have her dog with her or she can't fly.

Supervisor: That makes sense. You would be acting consistently with the ethical principles we mentioned. You're supporting her, being honest, and not causing harm to her or to society.

Trainee: But maybe I'm subtly causing her harm by reinforcing the idea that she cannot make this trip on her own and by showing her that I'll do whatever she wants so she won't have to deal with the difficult issues in therapy.

Supervisor: Good point. What can you do to minimize the likelihood of this sort of harm, other than simply refusing to write a factual letter?

Trainee: Well, I can write the letter, but I can explain the limits of what I can say, pointing out that we need to be accurate and truthful. I can tell her that I want to be helpful to her but that might also mean suggesting that she is capable of a higher level of functioning than she thinks, which might trigger her anxiety and mistrust at times.

Supervisor: Excellent. What else?

Trainee: I could tell her that there will undoubtedly be times when she and I won't see eye to eye, but that doesn't mean we can't work together benevolently or that we can't resolve our differences constructively.

Supervisor: Correct. Writing a factual letter this time does not mean that she has license to expect you to do whatever she wants, from now on, all the time! This situation can lead to an overt discussion about how she trusts or mistrusts others, how she views her level of self-efficacy, and how one can have a mature disagreement with someone else and not be harmed.

Trainee: It makes sense. This whole situation is an ethical issue as well as a therapeutic issue, and with a little problem-solving we can find a way to take constructive actions in both areas.

In this case, the supervisor leaves room for the supervisee to identify her own reactions and areas of discomfort with the situation before proposing a solution and uses the supervisee's own thought process as a framework for highlighting the ethical and therapeutic issues involved. Discussions such as this one can be a valuable method of facilitating supervisees' attunement to ethical issues and boosting their confidence in weighing such issues. Supervisors need to be able to recognize ethical issues when they occur in their supervisees' work; communicate their observations in a thoughtful, knowledgeable, nonsanctimonious way; engage in prompt problem solving when the need arises; and teach the supervisees how to *prevent* ethical problems from occurring or worsening. It is vitally important to create an atmosphere in supervision that is receptive to the open discussion of ethical issues, risks, and errors. Ideally, therapists-in-training should feel free to ask questions such as the following:

> "My client invited me to her wedding. I would hate to let her down by not going, but I'm not sure if it's appropriate. What should I do?"

"My client gave me a very nice gift; I tried to turn him down, but he insisted. Now I'm thinking that I need to return it to him, but I'm afraid of making him feel rejected, which is one of his vulnerabilities. Did I make a mistake in accepting the gift? Should I return it?"

"My client wants me to write him a letter that will explain that he missed some midterms owing to being 'too depressed' and asking for special accommodations for him to take them late. I'm uncomfortable doing this because the client never mentioned his exams until today, and frankly I doubt the legitimacy of my client's claims. I'm torn because I think it may be inappropriate for me to write this letter when it goes against my clinical opinion, but on the other hand my client is going to suffer some serious academic consequences if I decline. How should I handle this?"

"My client made an off-hand comment today that when her 14-year-old daughter came home after midnight, she was so angry that she 'throttled her.' I didn't ask what she meant by that, and now I'm thinking that I should have. Is this child abuse, and should I report it?"

"I think I made a big mistake, and I'm really worried about it. My client told me a lot of horror stories about her past hospitalizations, and then she made me promise that I would never hospitalize her again. I tried to empathize with her without really answering her, but I think I might have given her the impression that I wouldn't ever hospitalize her. How do I backpedal on this without totally losing her trust? Should I just keep the promise now that I think I made it, or would that endanger good clinical care in an emergency? Should I let this pass, and then just use my best judgment later if she needs to be hospitalized, even if she feels betrayed by me? I'm very confused. I'm really sorry about this. I know I should have handled this better."

These are but a small sample of the sorts of ethical questions that may arise in supervision. Our intent here is not to provide definitive answers to these questions because that often is not possible in the absence of context. Our message is that competent supervisors readily, humbly accept that they will need to help their supervisees flesh out issues such as these, weigh pros and cons, consider the case conceptualization and treatment plan in each instance, and perhaps consult further with outside parties (e.g., trusted colleagues, the director of the institutional program, members of state or provincial boards in the relevant mental health care field, the attorneys from one's liability insurance company). It is good practice to positively reinforce supervisees for bringing these matters to the supervisor's attention so that supervisees will be encouraged to face and address ethical dilemmas rather than overlook, underestimate, avoid, or (in a worst case scenario) simply disregard them. A particularly useful message to give supervisees about dealing with an ethical conundrum is that they rarely have to solve the problem immediately on the spot. It often is okay to defer responding and seek additional input from appropriate parties before reaching a conclusion with a definitive course of action. This approach reduces the risk of making impulsive or misinformed mistakes. It should be noted that sometimes it is quite appropriate for supervisors to consult with others as well.

INTERVENING DIRECTLY WITH THE CLIENT

Although it is important for supervisees to learn to handle independently a wide spectrum of clinical situations, there are times when it is appropriate and even necessary for supervisors to intervene directly with a supervisee's client (Newman, 2013). As the supervisor bears the ultimate clinical and legal responsibility for the client's care and as some clients pose a level of risk or high challenge that may exceed the supervisee's level of experience and/or competence, it is incumbent upon supervisors to get into the trenches and deal head-on with difficult clinical matters (Hipple & Beamish, 2007; Ladany, Friedlander, & Nelson, 2005). The benefits are many. Clients at risk gain additional clinical care, supervisees who are feeling alone and out of their depth gain the support of a trusted and experienced mentor, and the supervisor gains the chance to model important therapeutic and professional competencies. The following are several such direct intervention situations that we have faced, some of which were planned in advance following consultation with the supervisee and some of which occurred on the spur of the moment in an emergent crisis. In all cases, we met with the supervisees to process what had just occurred, toward the dual goals of ensuring proper follow-up with the clients and emphasizing what the supervisees learned from these situations. In each of the following illustrations, we use first-person pronouns without identifying which of us was involved, and client information is vague enough to preserve client anonymity.

Situation 1

A female practicum student therapist came to my office, saying that she had a male client who refused to leave her office until she gave him a hug (he was still there). We already knew from our previous supervision sessions that this client had a romantic attraction to the student therapist and a history of crossing boundaries inappropriately in many life situations, so his demand for a hug was not merely an innocent request for support at a difficult time. The student told me that she had another client waiting to be seen and didn't know what to do because her office was still occupied by the hug-demanding client who wouldn't leave. I told her to use my office to see her next client and that I would go into the office with the hug-demanding client to set firm limits with him and to reestablish the ground rules of the clinic to which he would have to adhere to continue as a client with us. Later, in a debriefing meeting with the practicum student, I inquired as to how she felt about continuing to work with this client, and she stated that she was willing to do so, confident in her ability to set limits. I gave her positive feedback for conceptualizing the situation well, not reinforcing the client's inappropriate behavior, consulting with me promptly, and having the fortitude to try working with the client anew.

Situation 2

A postdoctoral supervisee called me on my personal line after work hours, stating that one of her clients (in a clinical trial involving high-risk clients) had just called to leave a message that she was going to kill herself tonight. The postdoctoral therapist first called the client immediately, tried to assess if the client had already taken any self-harming actions, and (upon learning that she had not) instructed her to go to the emergency department of a nearby hospital or disclose her location so that the therapist could call the police to find her and transport her to the hospital. The client refused on both counts and hung up. She would not answer her phone when the postdoctoral therapist tried several times to call back. Upon learning of this situation, I instructed the postdoctoral therapist to refer to the client's intake information sheet, on which the client had listed her home address and emergency contact numbers, and call both a contact person and the police, letting both parties know that there was reasonable cause for immediate concern, stating that it was not clear if the client was at home; I also told the therapist to make herself available as the clinical contact person to continue to talk with the police as the situation developed. In the meantime, I called the client directly, in the hope that she would not recognize the incoming phone number and would answer out of curiosity, which she did. I identified myself to the client as her therapist's supervisor, engaged her in a discussion about how she was feeling and why she wanted to die, reaffirmed that her therapist (my supervisee) was concerned and wanted to do everything possible to help her and keep her safe, and said we were glad she had let us know about her suicidal intentions rather than simply acting on them. I kept her on the line until her good friend (the emergency contact person) and then the police arrived. I took full responsibility for this maneuver, apologized to the client for making the judgment call not to tell her that the police were on the way, and added that her therapist would be ready to resume outpatient treatment with her upon her safe and proper discharge from the hospital. In the debriefing with the postdoctoral therapist, we reestablished and updated a clinical treatment plan and prepared ourselves to meet together with the client (with my being there for only one session) upon her return to outpatient care.

Situation 3

My supervisee informed me that she had only just then learned from a medical school official who had previously referred a (now-ongoing) client that the client had a history of violence. This client often misused therapy sessions to rail against third parties for their acts of "injustice" and to make disparaging remarks toward women, including the therapist. He tended to dominate sessions with his angry complaints, and now he was demanding an official letter from the therapist "confirming" that he was well enough to return to medical school, which clearly he was not. The supervisee was concerned that if she told him that she could not write the letter, he might become violent toward her. I agreed to meet with this client along with the supervisee, and I called the client in advance to let him know that I (in my role as clinical supervisor) would be attending. I also called the police, explaining the situation (but without naming the client) and asking for an officer to be in the waiting room in plain clothes at the time of the scheduled session. The supervisee and I made a plan for how to run the session, in which I would confirm to the client that our clinic was committed to helping him with his psychological problems, but because he had not apprised us of his history of violence, we were not in a position to make any endorsements on his behalf until this issue had been dealt with thoroughly in therapy, which had not yet occurred. In planning for the session, I told the supervisee that if I thought the situation with the client was becoming potentially dangerous (e.g., if he were to become hostile in response to our comments), I would instruct her to leave the room so that I could talk to the client "in private," which would be her cue to alert the plainclothes policeman to come to the office at once. Thankfully, the situation never reached this level of crisis. Although the policeman was at the ready, the client simply balked at further therapy, stating that he would find somebody "more competent." He left, and we never heard from him again. We called him to follow up, and we left messages asking that he confirm that he was in treatment with someone else, but he never responded.

Situation 4

An advanced psychiatry resident in his CBT rotation explained in a supervision session that his client often tried to turn the therapeutic relationship into a "friendship" and that he was becoming hesitant to meet with her. He explained that she had made "flirtatious threats," saying that the rules for professional boundaries were "stupid," and that if he did not become her friend (e.g., including scheduling her for appointments after hours), she would in fact tell her friends and family that she was being "abandoned" in her treatment. The supervisee was at a loss as he wanted to maintain proper boundaries with this client, but he did not want his appropriate actions to result in his being accused of causing harm to a client. He also noted that he felt increasingly uncomfortable seeing this client but did not want to end treatment as that might in fact become a case of abandoning the client, thus adding credence to her threatened complaint. After discussing various options, all in the context of reviewing the case conceptualization for clues as to how to respond, we opted for a model in which we would provide this client with *dual provider care*, with the twist being that we would be in the room at the same time for every session. The goal was to provide this client with the treatment she needed (i.e., not abandoning her) while greatly reducing the sense of *intimacy* she was trying to create while meeting one on one with the male resident. In addition, I explained to the client that it was my decision (as the supervisor) to change the parameters of treatment, and I gave her a thorough rationale, all the while taking great pains not to scold or shame her. At first, the client was unhappy with this cotherapy arrangement, but she adapted, and treatment proceeded until the end of the resident's rotation. I then transferred the client's care to a female resident.

One of the not-so-obvious challenges for supervisors in scenarios of the sort described is how to be empathic with clients with whom they have never worked (or bonded) directly, all while setting limits, usually under some duress. We as supervisors may consider ourselves to be fully capable of being empathic on demand, but it couldn't hurt to go the extra mile by preparing ourselves mentally and emotionally for such situations, just to make sure that we bring our best interpersonal skills to bear on the matter. This may take the form of being self-reflective about any negative automatic thoughts we may be having at those times when we have to intervene and responding rationally in advance of making contact with the supervisee's client. Examples of such rational responses could be the following:

> "My supervisee has worked hard to create a good connection with this client, and I want to preserve that."
>
> "This may be extra work for me, but it's also a great opportunity to be a positive role model for my trainee about acting professionally in a difficult situation."
>
> "My supervisee needs my support at a time like this, and I intend to come through."
>
> "I intend to set limits with my supervisee's client, but the first thing I'm going to ask the client is how he's feeling, and I'm going to listen."

Supervisors would do well to remember that their supervisees typically are working hard to establish and maintain their positive therapeutic relationship with their clients, so the supervisors' direct interactions with the clients need to be congruent with the goal of supporting their supervisees in this important endeavor.

As one may easily ascertain from the length and breadth of this chapter, *special* issues in supervision are many and varied, driving home the point that supervision is not just about teaching CBT. The job of a competent CBT supervisor is demanding and often complicated, requiring ongoing self-monitoring and continuing education throughout one's career.

5

Supervisor Development and Self-Care

TRAINING AND DEVELOPMENT OF THE SUPERVISOR

Unlike days of yore, when learning the nuts and bolts of doing clinical supervision was an *on-the-job training* scenario (see Newman, 2013), it is now acknowledged that the training of supervisors needs to be formalized, and it needs to start before supervisors actually work with supervisees. Ideally, such training would take place during the advanced years of graduate school, perhaps after the trainees have successfully completed a couple of years of practicum work as a cognitive–behavioral therapy (CBT) practitioner-in-training. At that point, these students would have enough familiarity with the CBT approach to know what constitutes competency in this model in particular and how to measure client progress and outcomes in general. At the same time, these students would not yet be sufficiently credentialed to provide "real" supervision (with all its attendant responsibilities and medical–legal mandates), so they would

http://dx.doi.org/10.1037/14950-006
Supervision Essentials for Cognitive–Behavioral Therapy, by C. F. Newman and D. A. Kaplan

need to take part in *simulated* supervision scenarios, such as role-playing (perhaps as a structured part of a graduate seminar on supervision), and group supervision, in which the students would be encouraged by the group leader (i.e., the professional who is licensed or the *meta-supervisor* of the group) to give each other feedback on their management of their cases.

Several models for the training of supervisors have been developed (see Milne, Sheikh, Pattison, & Wilkinson, 2011), a thorough review of which would go well beyond the scope of this concise text. Nevertheless, let us take a brief look at two such models. One model, geared toward established professionals seeking continuing education, holds that a combination of interactive workshops (involving video clips and role-playing), written materials (e.g., handouts, scoring codes, and/or a manual), plus ongoing metasupervision (perhaps via phone or computer) is a robust method for helping professionals practice and maintain their new competencies in conducting supervision (Beidas & Kendall, 2010). Workshops alone are a good starting point, but without supplemental learning materials, ongoing mentoring, and planned self-reflection (see Bennett-Levy & Padesky, 2014), there is a tendency for the workshop participants to revert quickly back to their customary practices (Miller, Yahne, Moyers, Martinez, & Pirritano, 2004; Rakovshik & McManus, 2010; Sholomskas et al., 2005). One such comprehensive program of supervisor development is the Advanced Cognitive Therapy Studies program at the Oxford Cognitive Therapy Centre (https://www.octc.co.uk) offered in five, spaced workshops. Among these short courses are those that focus on learning to be a CBT supervisor and trainer; the classes involve between-course assignments and evaluations by the senior psychologists of the Centre.

A second model, aimed at advanced graduate students who are still learning to be therapists and are not yet credentialed, involves formal course work (as part of the requirement for the terminal degree) over a semester or a year. A formal course as part of graduate training allows for ample repetitions of multimodal teaching methods, including a reading list, classroom discussion of such readings, classroom viewing of audio-visual recordings of CBT sessions with participatory *color commentary* supervision (e.g., where both the therapist featured on the recording and the others in the class weigh in on their views about what is transpiring on the video), learning to use established scales to rate such recordings (e.g., the Cognitive Therapy Rating Scale [CTRS], Young & Beck, 1980), and role-playing. Regarding this latter element of training, the role-playing may occur in triads, in which one of the students provides supervision of a dyadic therapy role-play, or with the course instructor being the fourth person who serves as a *metasupervisor* who then gives feedback to the supervisor after the triadic exercise is complete.

One of us instructed a supervision training seminar for advanced students in a CBT-oriented clinical psychology doctoral program (Newman, 2013) that was divided into training modules (involving respective sets of readings and assignments), as follows:

1. Overview of the chief responsibilities and competencies of being a clinical supervisor.
2. The supervisory relationship.
3. Being conversant in and sensitive to ethical and cross-cultural issues in supervision.
4. Maximizing trainee competency in CBT (and doing CTRS ratings).
5. Documentation, feedback-giving, and the evaluative role of the supervisor.
6. Managing supervisees' work with high-risk clients and crises.

The seminar included live practice sessions involving instructor modeling, role-playing, and feedback from both the class and the course instructor. Note that many of the foundational (i.e., professionwide) competencies of supervision were taught first, before the teaching of functional competencies (i.e., specific to the methods of CBT) in the fourth module, the latter of which required considerable time and attention.

Aside from the readings, course assignments often involved the graduate students creating audiovisual recordings of their CBT sessions with real clients and viewing, rating, and discussing them later in class. In other words, the students would rate their own work as CBT therapists as if they were their own supervisors, giving themselves constructive feedback on such variables as their structuring of sessions, use of homework, the quality of their alliance-building skills, using a case formulation to devise a strategy for change, focusing on key client behaviors and cognitions, using CBT techniques and guided discovery questioning, eliciting feedback, and the like. The instructor also showed audiovisual recordings of his own work with CBT clients and encouraged the class to critique and rate those sessions, too! In this manner, the course instructor was acting as a "coping model," a highly effective way to model personal development and the learning of skills (Bandura, 1986), destigmatize the idea of making mistakes, and encourage students to self-assess and self-improve in the same way (see Calhoun, Moras, Pilkonis, & Rehm, 1998). With a little encouragement and not too much cajoling, the students soon began to practice their supervisory skills on the course instructor without undue inhibition. The atmosphere was one of collegiality, in which feedback was offered to help whoever was being evaluated as a CBT practitioner.

It is important to state that the course modules on cross-cultural and ethical issues in supervision, as well as supervising the care of high-risk clients, were not meant to provide any sort of *definitive word* on the subjects. These important areas of concern often involve significant gray zones, generally requiring an understanding of situational context and customarily benefiting from additional consultation. Thus, lively class discussions were held about numerous hypothetical supervisory situations, under the heading, "If you were the supervisor, how would you handle this?" A few examples included the following:

- Your supervisee asks you if it's okay for him to accept a gift from a client.
- Your supervisee is of Hispanic descent. You receive a direct call from her client, stating that he wants his care to be transferred "to a therapist who is white."
- Your supervisee states, "I'm trying to help my client modify her all-or-none dysfunctional belief that her family will disown her if she tells them that she is seriously dating a boyfriend who is of a different religion, but she's not changing."

- Your supervisee says, "Working with my client Mr. X feels creepy and unsafe."
- You have a supervisee who is South Asian, and you wish to assign her a new client who also happens to be South Asian. You assume that they will be a good match, but is that necessarily so?
- You are meeting with your supervisee when it suddenly occurs to you that you have not discussed one of her chronically suicidal clients in some time. You ask the supervisee about this, and she replies that the client "dropped out of treatment."

Classroom discussions on these (and other) hypothetical supervisory situations help trainees learn to think like supervisors, which involves being willing to take responsibility for providing competent professional guidance to trainees and knowing when it is wise to consult with others. This sort of supervision training course also helps the students to be more aware of the important topics they need to be discussing with their own current clinical supervisors, including preventing and/or dealing with high-risk situations, hashing out ethical dilemmas, and tuning in to cultural biases that may be subtly influencing therapy and/or supervision. When this happens, all parties involved in the training of the students (and the students themselves) have to raise the bar for themselves, which ultimately benefits clients.

ONGOING LEARNING AND CONSULTATION FOR THE SUPERVISOR AND METASUPERVISION

Becoming a supervisor in CBT is not an *outcome* but rather the start of a career-long process. To continue to develop and grow as professionals—and to transcend from competence to true expertise—supervisors need to self-monitor their work and occasionally seek consultation from qualified others. Consultation may take the form of a periodic meeting of supervisors within an organization or clinic, serving the dual functions of peer supervision (e.g., keeping each other from drifting off their supervisory protocol) and administrative problem solving (e.g., how best to address one of their graduate students who is struggling in practicum work). More formally, consultation may involve *supervision of supervision*, also known as *metasupervision* (Newman, 2013), in which a highly experienced CBT supervisor provides oversight and feedback to a more junior supervisor (or to a supervisor less experienced in CBT per se). The junior supervisor bears the clinical and legal responsibility for the therapist's training and the well-being of the clients, whereas the metasupervisor facilitates the junior supervisor's self-reflection rather than issuing orders. As Barton (2015) aptly stated, "A learning community is not a chain of command." The metasupervisor endeavors to help the supervisor trainees to improve their supervision skills in general, expand and deepen their CBT supervision repertoire in particular, receive formal evaluations for credentialing purposes (e.g., being designated as an expert supervisor in the Academy of Cognitive Therapy [http://www.academyofct.org]), and receive additional guidance in managing the cases that are being seen under the supervisor trainees' umbrella of clinical responsibility.

Metasupervision can also help improve the working relationship between supervisors and their supervisees, helping them to collaborate more effectively and thus helping everyone, most importantly the clients. An excellent illustration is provided by Armstrong and Freeston (2006), who described a case in which the supervisor and supervisee clashed over their different approaches to the handling of a case. The supervisor valued case conceptualization and thus wanted the supervisee to be more thoughtful and mindful about matching interventions to the specific, unique needs of the client. The supervisee, by contrast, felt institutional pressure to help clients make progress quickly to facilitate client turnover in the clinic and thus wanted to focus on teaching the client some general coping skills right away. As the authors noted, a metasupervisor observing this problem in supervision would be in an excellent position to give the supervisor helpful feedback, perhaps highlighting the need for better goal congruence and advising the supervisor to recognize and empathize with the supervisee's sense of performance pressure. The metasupervisor might then initiate a role-play exercise so that the supervisor could practice a congenial way of addressing the need to combine the teaching of CBT skills with attention to conceptualization issues in therapy. The supervisor may then be well-prepared to repair the strain in the supervisory relationship, improve communication in the supervision session, and facilitate an improved sense of shared purpose in helping the clients.

Another example of the utility of metasupervision doubles as a reminder of the importance of striving toward cultural competency in conducting cognitive–behavioral supervision (CBS), as described in Newman (2013). The metasupervisor was a male, U.S.-based psychologist providing formal oversight for a male, Asian psychiatrist who was training in CBS as part of an international training program (the Beck Institute for Cognitive Behavior Therapy, http://www.beckinstitute.org). The U.S.-based metasupervisor observed a video of the Asian psychiatrist (held in the latter's home office in the Far East) meeting with a female supervisee (a psychiatry resident). The two Asian professionals held their supervision session in English for the benefit of the U.S.-based metasupervisor. They discussed the case of a client who exhibited significant levels of anxiety and avoidance and whose treatment plan included planned exposure exercises, a well-established, empirically supported intervention. Unfortunately, as the supervising psychiatrist and his resident explained on the video, the client did not wish to do the imaginal exposures that had been proposed as a homework assignment, and the resident decided to honor his request to sidestep the assignment, at least temporarily. The supervising psychiatrist skillfully helped the resident to conceptualize the client's problematic avoidance, express empathy for the client, and yet find a way to motivate the client to take graded steps toward doing the exposures. The resident quietly, politely agreed to do this in the next session.

The U.S.-based metasupervisor gave high marks to the supervising psychiatrist for his professionalism and competence in managing the supervision session with his resident, but added a culturally based question. He noted that the resident had spoken slowly, quietly, and politely in the supervision session as she agreed with the supervisor to press on with helping the client to face the imaginal exposure exercises. The U.S.-based metasupervisor then wondered aloud if the resident was in a bit of a bind in that she might be trying to be deferential and respectful toward her older, male client (who did *not* wish to take part in the planned intervention) and now was trying to be deferential and respectful toward her older, male supervisor who was encouraging her to go *ahead* with the exposure interventions. The U.S.-based metasupervisor interpreted the female supervisee's quiet, demure manner as being supportive of this hypothesis. The metasupervisor also respectfully added that he was not implying that a young Asian woman (especially a highly credentialed one) would necessarily be passive and deferential to older Asian men, but at the same time he did not want to miss a potentially culturally related phenomenon. Thus, the metasupervisor brought up this topic tentatively, eager to obtain the psychiatrist supervisor's opinion on this issue.

The Asian supervisor nicely corrected the U.S.-based metasupervisor on this matter, saying that there was ample evidence that the resident supervisee had been quite capable of managing the client in terms of setting limits and organizing the sessions and that she had at times been able to express opinions in supervision that differed somewhat from those offered by the supervisor. Thus, the supervisor was confident that the supervisee was not in a culturally based double bind of the sort that the U.S.-based metasupervisor hypothesized.

Later, the U.S.-based metasupervisor described this situation as part of a lecture to mental health professionals in another Asian locale. These Asian clinicians offered an additional hypothesis that the metasupervisor had not considered. They hypothesized that the resident supervisee may have been considerably more animated and vocal if she had been speaking in her native language, as she was accustomed to doing in supervision. The fact that she was going out of her way to take part in that particular supervision session in English may have been a significant factor in making her look quiet and passive. This idea had never occurred to the metasupervisor, and he realized (once again) how difficult it can be to be culturally sensitive in doing international training and how easy it is to fall back on Anglo-centric assumptions about language. Nonetheless, the course of metasupervision between the U.S.-based psychologist and the Asian psychiatrist was productive, and the latter stated that the guidance and validation he received had been beneficial to his work with his resident.

SUPERVISOR WELLNESS

As meaningful and rewarding as the work of a CBT clinician can be, the responsibilities of being a therapist and/or supervisor can be daunting and stressful. To be healthy role models for supervises and clients and to be functioning properly in our professional roles, we need to make our own wellness a priority, perhaps by utilizing the coping skills we teach others. When therapists actively self-apply CBT methods, they gain valuable technical practice and promote a better sense of empathy for their clients regarding the trial-and-error process of learning to make cognitive–behavioral changes. They also improve their own morale and sense of self-efficacy in the process. Therapists who use CBT skills for themselves may also be more adept at remaining empathic when at first their thoughts may otherwise lead them to be angry with their clients as they are able to recognize and moderate their own emotional reactions in the moment (see Newman, 2012). This sort of *self-reflective* practice is an essential part of developing expertise in conducting CBT (Bennett-Levy et al., 2015).

The process of therapist self-application of CBT techniques begins with clinical supervisors fostering the development of their trainees' self-reflection skills. Supervisors can do this best by creating a safe, accepting environment in which their trainees can share their own automatic thoughts (e.g., about their own work or how they feel about their clients) without fear of disapproval (Newman, 2013). With practice, the CBT trainees then become that much more adept at encouraging their clients to self-reflect in a similar way, thus leading to more productive therapy sessions and a better transfer of skills to the clients.

Supervisor wellness is closely related to wellness as a therapist. Both positions involve a high level of responsibility, exposures to many clinical stories that can be heartrending, being a potential lightning rod for the negative feelings of those you are sincerely trying to help, and having your work exposed and scrutinized firsthand as the norm. Maintaining wellness as a clinician—whether as a supervisor or a supervisee—involves being able to self-apply the methods of CBT to keep things in perspective (rather than catastrophize), stay in problem-solving mode (rather than feeling helpless and avoiding), learn and grow from negative experiences (i.e., come to accept, tolerate, and even embrace discomfort in the service of the great value of becoming a better clinician), be mindful of the meaningful moments that so frequently occur in the course of one's work (i.e., feeling honored and privileged to be trusted and held in high regard and to bear witness to others' pathways to personal growth), and *balance* all of these aspects with personal pursuits that allow one to recharge one's personal battery, feel nurtured and refreshed, and immerse oneself in a wide range of life experiences. Aside from that, there's nothing to it!

There are methods that CBT practitioners and supervisors can practice during a busy, stressful day that can help promote wellness and enhance clinical performance. For example, a brief mindfulness exercise before a therapy or supervision session can be a boon to the clinician's alertness and effectiveness. In a randomized trial, Dunn, Callahan, Swift, and Ivanovic (2013) showed that therapists who engaged in a 5-minute "centering exercise" (from *Acceptance and Commitment Therapy: An Experiential Approach to Behavior Change* [Hayes, Strosahl, & Wilson, 1999]) before meeting with a client rated themselves as being more present in the subsequent session, and the clients also rated the sessions more favorably. Anecdotally, we have recommended that our trainees generate and think of self-statements that promote hope and self-support, particularly in the context of treating high-risk, high-maintenance clients who test our mettle, patience, and the limits of our professional coping. Such self-statements, which can be practiced before sessions as well as *during* sessions (silently, to oneself), include

- "My client may not accept my expressions of goodwill or collaborate with my best efforts to provide helpful interventions, but I will offer them just the same."
- "Don't take [the client's negative comments] personally. It's all data. Conceptualize the problem, and respond in a professional manner that exceeds the client's expectations."
- "My worth as a therapist does not hinge on this one client's response to treatment. I will continue to make a good faith effort to provide the best CBT I can. I have helped others, and I must not forget that. Perhaps I can still help this client, too."

Similarly, supervisors can catch their own automatic thoughts, and respond to them therapeutically, as illustrated by the following examples:

Automatic Thought: I hate having to give my supervisee critical feedback for his struggles in doing CBT and keeping up with the notes. This meeting is going to be so painful today.

Rational Response: I can be thoughtful and respectful when I share my concerns with him. I can ask for feedback. I can show that his progress in this program is a priority. I can model how to be collaborative when talking about uncomfortable topics, which is something he needs to learn in working with his clients anyway. I can feel proud of myself for not postponing this meeting and for actively practicing antiavoidance.

Automatic Thought: I have too many supervisees and too many clients for whom I am responsible, and I'm just too tired to do it all. But that won't matter at all, and nobody will care about how I feel if there is an adverse incident. It will still be my failure.

Rational Response: You're tired, that's true, but not *too* tired to still be a skilled, caring professional who takes your work as a supervisor and therapist seriously. Rather than catastrophizing about possible adverse incidents, do some problem solving first. At least two of your colleagues have asked you if they can help in some way, and you always say no. Talk to them, and see what can be worked out in terms of reducing your supervisory load.

Such self-application of rational responding, problem solving, and reaching out to helpful others is good practice and good role-modeling. It reduces stress, and allows one's perception of the considerable upside of being a CBT supervisor to shine through more clearly.

6

Research Support for the Supervisory Approach and Future Directions

The status of cognitive–behavioral supervision (CBS) has advanced significantly during the last 20 years such that

> There is now a series of compelling and empirically supported recommendations as to best practices in [cognitive–behavioral therapy] CBT supervision that can be gleaned from competency sets, systematic reviews of supervision, and reviews of training and supervision in clinical trials that have demonstrated effectiveness. (Reiser, 2014, pp. 502–503)

Some of these best practices include making use of experiential methods such as role-playing that enhance procedural learning, direct observation of the behaviors of both supervisees (with clients) and supervisors (with their supervisees), the use of homework to enhance the transfer and maintenance of skills, and the measurement of progress and outcomes (of

http://dx.doi.org/10.1037/14950-007

both the trainees and their clients), among others (e.g., structuring sessions, using guided discovery questions, conceptualizing clinical problems). Part of this advancement has stemmed from the emphasis on developing psychometrically sound instruments with which to measure the mentoring behaviors of supervisors and the clinical behaviors of supervisees in their sessions with clients. A key goal is to determine which supervisor behaviors are most efficacious in training supervisees in CBT, then codifying these behaviors into manuals and studying the best ways to train supervisors in the use of such manuals for better dissemination (Reiser & Milne, 2012). These are challenging tasks, and although the current state of the field is promising, much work remains to be done.

MEASURES AND OUTCOMES

As noted, the field's ability to evaluate the efficacy of supervisory practices depends in part on there being reliable and valid ways of measuring the process. Similar to the codification and measurement of treatment adherence and competency, the assessment of the efficacy of CBS may utilize circumscribed manuals (perhaps in conjunction with treatment programs that use therapy manuals), or perhaps CBS will take a more principle-based approach, without necessarily specifying which discrete supervisory actions need to occur in which meetings.

The literature includes several excellent reviews of (and sources pertaining to) the empirical status of measures of therapist competence in delivering CBT (e.g., Muse & McManus, 2013) and of supervisor competence in mentoring trainees in becoming effective CBT practitioners (e.g., Milne & Reiser, 2011; Watkins & Milne, 2014). In addition, the Corrie and Lane (2015) book includes a copy of an additional promising measure (The Supervisor Evaluation Scale; Corrie & Worrell, 2012), and the Oxford Cognitive Therapy Centre has developed and tested an easy-to-use inventory for routinely rating supervisors' behaviors (The Supervisor Competency Scale; see Rakovshik, 2015). The reader is directed to these publications for a more complete overview of the state of the field. For the sake of brevity, we focus here on a widely used measure of CBT competence to which we have referred many times (the Cognitive Therapy Rating Scale [CTRS]) and a comprehensive, well-researched measure of supervisor competence called "SAGE" (Supervision: Adherence and Guidance Evaluation; Milne, Reiser, Cliffe, & Raine, 2011).

The Cognitive Therapy Rating Scale

Originally designed by Young and Beck (1980) to measure therapists' fidelity and competency in conducting cognitive therapy for depression, the CTRS, as well as its revised version (Blackburn et al., 2001), have been used to evaluate the delivery of Beckian CBT for a full spectrum of clinical problems. Clinically and administratively, the CTRS has also been used to evaluate supervisors' adherence to the CBT model and as a measure of readiness to conduct CBS at a proficient level. For example, although CTRS scores of 36, 39, and 40 (on a scale of 0–66) have been used respectively in various settings and protocols as threshold scores for competency as a CBT practitioner (see McManus, Rakovshik, Kennerley, Fennell, & Westbrook, 2012), the Beck Institute for Cognitive Behavior Therapy requires two ratings at a score of 50 or greater as a criterion for admission into its extramural training program for supervisors. Although we have already noted that treatment and supervision in CBT have much in common, and indeed there are items on the CTRS that are directly applicable to best practices in CBS (e.g., setting an agenda, collaboration, pacing, interpersonal effectiveness, focusing on key cognitions and behaviors, having a conceptualization-based strategy for change, eliciting feedback, assigning homework), the CTRS does not explicitly rate some items that have been identified as being part of evidence-based supervision (e.g., using multimodal methods of teaching, using video observations and ratings); thus, the CTRS does not map onto supervision optimally. On the other hand, there is evidence that when the CTRS is used regularly in supervision, the supervisees' clients have better outcomes (Simons et al., 2010), an example of the benefits of ongoing measurement of supervisees' progress.

Although the CTRS is widely used and frequently studied (Trepka, Rees, Shapiro, Hardy, & Barkham, 2004), both versions have had mixed results in terms of interrater reliability (Muse & McManus, 2013). Thus, one of the future directions in the study of measuring practitioner competency in CBT (one of the central responsibilities of supervisors) will be further refinement and study of the CTRS and similar measures, without which the links among supervisor competency, therapist competency, and client outcome will be difficult to ascertain clearly (see Webb, DeRubeis, & Barber, 2010).

Supervision: Adherence and Guidance Evaluation (SAGE)

The SAGE scale for rating supervisor competence in CBT has a lengthy history of conceptual and methodological development (see Milne & Reiser, 2014). SAGE includes 22 items on which a supervisor is quantitatively evaluated on a scale of 0–6 (from absent to expertly done, much like the CTRS) across three larger domains. One of these domains is dubbed "common factors" and includes items such as interpersonal relating and collaborating. A second domain is called the "supervision cycle" and features items such as agenda setting, feedback (giving and receiving), evaluating, questioning, listening, and teaching. The third domain is known as the "supervisee cycle," with scoring items such as conceptualizing and planning. Notably, the rater (who essentially serves as a metasupervisor) also can offer qualitative written feedback to provide a rationale for a rating, give specific suggestions for improvement, or offer positive comments. SAGE includes a scoring manual, according to which, "[T]he instrument can be used to evaluate the competence of supervisors; to audit adherence to standards for supervision (especially CBS); to develop practice, by enabling detailed feedback to be provided to supervisors; and to profile different styles of supervision" (Milne & Reiser, 2014, p. 410). SAGE is actively being used in numerous ongoing studies. In terms of future directions, this scoring system undoubtedly will play an important role in the further empirical development of guidelines for competent CBS, as well as in studies on the impact of CBS on supervisees and their clients. Milne (2014) has developed, as a companion to SAGE, a complementary 11-item questionnaire called REACT (Rating of Experiential Learning and

Components of Teaching & Supervision) that solicits supervisees' feedback. Similar to SAGE, REACT allows for the collection of quantitative and qualitative data. The psychometric data on REACT have been good, making this another promising measure for ongoing and future research.

Recent literature reviews of the research on clinical supervision have shown that much of the extant work has focused on the *process* of supervision more than the *outcomes* (e.g., Pilling & Roth, 2014; Roth & Pilling, 2008b). The link between supervisor competency and favorable client outcomes has been a challenge to demonstrate systematically (see Bambling, King, Raue, Schweitzer, & Lambert, 2006), although there is more evidence for each link in the chain, in that competent supervision improves the supervisees' clinical competencies (e.g., enhancing their alliance-building, interviewing, and technical skills, see Beinart, 2014; Inman et al., 2014; Mannix et al., 2006; Reiser, 2014; Roth & Pilling, 2008b), and there is evidence that therapists who demonstrate better CBT competencies produce better outcomes for clients receiving CBT (e.g., Brown et al., 2013; Ginzburg et al., 2012; Kuyken & Tsivrikos, 2009; Strunk, Brotman, DeRubeis, & Hollon, 2010; Trepka et al., 2004). In fact, the Mannix et al. (2006) randomized, controlled trial showed that competent CBS could be used effectively in a cross-disciplinary fashion. In this landmark study involving the training and supervision of palliative care nurses in delivering CBT coping techniques to patients with cancer, the authors found that continuation of supervision of one group of nurses resulted in significantly better performance of their core CBT skills and maintenance of self-confidence as CBT clinicians when compared to the nurses assigned to the group whose supervision discontinued after 6 months. All of the nurses in the study earlier had shown significant skill attainment in the first 6 months of the project, in which everyone received the equivalent of 12 days of CBT instruction and skills-building supervision. From these findings, the authors concluded that in this cohort of nurses, supervision was necessary to ensure maintenance of their CBT skills and the confidence to use them.

As challenging as it has been to find causal links from supervisor behavior to client outcomes, some data exist that give us reason to be optimistic about our ability to identify the key elements of supervisor competency and determine the impact of supervisory behaviors on trainee performance and client progress. For example, in a quantitative and qualitative content analysis of the *transfer of impact* from CBS to CBT practice, 20 audio recordings of 10 alternating supervision and therapy sessions suggested that "[S]upervision clearly and repeatedly improved patient care, albeit within an uncontrolled n = 1 design" (Milne, Pilkington, Gracie, & James, 2003, cited in Milne, 2014, pp. 52–53). Milne (2014) reviewed numerous randomized controlled trials conducted in the United Kingdom and Australia and found supervision was associated with improved client care and outcomes, but he urged caution in determining a causal link, in that supervisor behaviors were not sufficiently measured and fidelity to a CBT approach could not be confirmed. Milne suggested that future studies on the efficacy of CBS would do well to place more emphasis on its design, delivery, and impact on supervisee learning and enactment than on client outcomes per se, arguing that client variables add considerable statistical noise in trying to evaluate the level of competency of the supervision originating at the start of the causal chain (also see Reiser & Milne, 2014).

The phenomena of measures that are not yet as psychometrically sound as they could be combined with the high variability of client functioning and engagement make it difficult to firmly link therapist competency with client outcome when evaluating one clinician at a time. This problem has been remedied somewhat through larger sample sizes, such as in evaluating an entire training program or interpreting the results of a large-scale outcome study (Muse & McManus, 2013; Webb et al., 2010). The use of larger samples would be helpful in allowing the field to state more confidently that when supervisors adhere to evidence-based practices, their supervisees consequently adhere more closely to the treatment protocol (Inman et al., 2014) and that positively rated supervisory relationships are related to better supervisee development and learning (Beinart, 2014).

Let us now turn our attention to some current developments in the field that are informing us about future directions, including (a) the routine, formalized early training of supervisors; (b) dissemination and evaluation of supervision methods that are global in scope; (c) expanded oversight of supervision practices across the professional lifespan; and (d) more comprehensive and secure use of technology (with clear, corresponding professional guidelines).

ROUTINE, FORMALIZED, EARLY TRAINING OF SUPERVISORS

The field of clinical supervision has come a long way since the days when new supervisors had their first exposure to "training" when they began working with their first supervisees. The field has recognized that formal instruction is a necessary prerequisite for optimally conducting supervision (American Psychological Association and Commission on Accreditation, 2009) and that the contents of such instruction need to be derived from evidence-based practices in the modality of therapy being supervised. Research on best practices in supervision is an area that is only now starting to grow, but over time there will be an ever-growing database on which to construct supervision programs that are efficacious in shaping the clinical skills of therapists-in-training. Ultimately, the aim is to show that early, systematic training in supervision will produce better supervisors, which in turn will lead to more competent therapists, which will result in healthier, more durable therapeutic outcomes for clients.

As the future brings more studies on supervision, the result will be a broader evidence base on which to construct training courses on best practices. In the years to come, graduate level training in supervision will no longer feel like a new frontier but will become more firmly embedded in the normative early-career curriculum. Therapists-in-training will simultaneously be supervisors-in-training, and through this more demanding apprenticeship, they will become more knowledgeable about the key ingredients of the supervision they receive. The bar will naturally be set higher for all parties because long-time supervisors will need to keep up with advancements in the field to satisfy their more aware trainees, and the trainees will be better positioned to accept and adapt to the professional demands of being fully licensed and credentialed. All of this should result in improvements in the delivery of CBT to the clients, which we anticipate will be confirmed by the data in the years ahead.

DISSEMINATION AND EVALUATION OF SUPERVISION METHODS THAT ARE GLOBAL IN SCOPE

Cognitive–behavioral therapy, as a modality originally rooted in cultures in which English was the primary language, requires modifications appropriate to nonanglophone and non-Western cultures if it is to be used worldwide. Over the past few decades, the promulgation of promising data from a plethora of CBT clinical trials, coupled with sociological, political, and technological changes that have rapidly changed the world, have resulted in the widespread establishment of academic and clinical centers for CBT around the globe. Indeed, hubs of CBT exist on six continents (and it is not out of the question that there will someday be a CBT center in Antarctica for lonely, worried scientists and environmentalists).

As the field continues to be more aware of cultural adaptations that need to be made to CBT conceptualization and intervention (see Hays & Iwamasa, 2006; Tsui, O'Donoghue, & Ng, 2014), there is an ever-growing need to train and credential supervisors whose practice largely will not be in English. Organizations such as the Academy of Cognitive Therapy (ACT, http://www.academyofct.org), in part through their international listserv, have begun to involve a more multicultural, multilingual cohort of experienced clinicians around the world to serve as supervisors and metasupervisors when therapy sessions are conducted across the linguistic spectrum. For example, when an applicant includes a recording of a CBT session as part of his or her submission for credentialing by the ACT, it is becoming more likely that it can be evaluated and formally rated by a senior clinician who will be able to understand the language directly, without having to risk skewing the meanings via an attempted translation into English.

As noted, the acquisition of cross-cultural knowledge and related clinical competency is a lifelong endeavor. Thus, at any given point in time, both supervisors and their supervisees will be in the process of learning about the normative belief systems and behavioral practices of clients from a wide range of heritages and locales, as well as gaining awareness of variations in international codes of ethics (Thomas, 2014). The ongoing increase in international training opportunities (coupled with the technology to enact secure supervision from a distance) will necessitate that supervisors learn from their supervisees when it comes to adapting CBT for use with the latters' clients. Far from viewing this as a *complication* in the process of training, competent CBT supervisors will embrace this opportunity for bidirectional, synergistic learning.

Cross-cultural issues also play a role in international collaborative research projects, in which coinvestigators need to take into account the effects of using measures (both self-report and observational ratings of others) that have been adapted for use in different languages and contrasting societies. As a humorous anecdote, Milne and Reiser (2014) describe the culture gap that can exist even when both researchers share a common mother tongue. When Milne (from the United Kingdom) used SAGE to rate the supervision sessions of Reiser (from the United States), the former found the latter's upbeat, can-do attitude a bit at odds with the common British style of understatement, and it could well have adversely affected the ratings if Milne had not been alert to this cultural difference. Notably, in the spirit of the notion that "everybody is a student," Milne humbly added that he learned in the process of doing the qualitative ratings of Reiser's supervision sessions "to try and be a notch or two more positive" (p. 411).

IMPROVED AND EXPANDED OVERSIGHT OF SUPERVISION PRACTICES ACROSS THE PROFESSIONAL LIFESPAN

As the field further responds to the need for more training, practice, and research on supervision, accrediting and licensing boards will routinely mandate supervisors to demonstrate their periodic participation in continuing education on this subject. In addition, more professionals will have the opportunity to take part in research trials of supervision, thus offering them greater exposure to training along with metasupervision. Graduate training programs will prioritize the regular convening of supervisors' meetings, the collection of students' evaluations of supervisors, and the recording of supervision sessions for oversight and future training purposes. Over time, this will become the norm.

Training in CBS now is being offered sooner in one's career than it had been in earlier epochs. Therefore, accreditation bodies evaluating graduate programs in mental health fields will evaluate such programs' adherence to high standards in introducing students to the basics of being a supervisor. At the other end of the timeline, maintaining one's license to practice will necessitate confirmation of ongoing, updated training in best practices in supervision.

MORE ROUTINE AND SECURE USE OF TECHNOLOGY WITH CONSENSUS GUIDELINES

As described in detail by Rousmaniere (2014), "The past two decades has [sic] witnessed an explosion in the number of technologies being used to deliver and enhance supervision and training, such as Web-based videoconference . . . Web-based software for tracking clinical outcomes, and software to code psychotherapy session videos" (p. 204). As a result, supervision and training from great distances is rapidly becoming commonplace, and this trend will only become more pronounced, especially as a way to reduce travel costs, reach clinicians in remote areas, and improve assessment of outcomes (e.g., in terms of therapist-acquired competencies and client wellness). Rousmaniere (2014) also noted that these advancements bring with them a host of questions and challenges of the practical and legal–ethical variety that are nowhere close to being resolved at present. For example, how can supervisors maintain the confidentiality of client records if they have access to them via mobile devices and/or "the cloud"? To what degree will technological competency be a necessary supervisory competency for the proper use of new devices and methods for safely receiving, transmitting, storing, and deleting sensitive clinical material? How will distance supervision affect the supervisory relationship and related client outcomes? How can clients best be given accurate, comprehensible, and perhaps frequent updates about how their personal information will be communicated and protected so that the clients' consent can truly be "informed?"

These are the sorts of questions that will receive more attention over time, not only in academic discussions but also in terms of new policies and mandates that will need periodic updating.

These and other questions are being tackled to some extent, and Rousmaniere (2014) offers useful suggestions on choosing cloud-based file storage and transfer services—as well as telepsychology programs— that are compliant with the Health Insurance Portability and Accountability Act (HIPAA) in the United States. He also highlights the hazards of assuming that such services, devices, and programs are discrete, single-purpose, only turned on when used, and "private" (as opposed to public) as the default mode. He proposes that supervisors will need to assume quite the opposite—that sensitive client information is part of a *technology ecosystem* unless steps are actively taken to isolate such information (e.g., via strong passwords, encryption, privacy settings deliberately set to "private"). In the United States, the American Psychological Association (APA) has published the "Guidelines for the Practice of Telepsychology" (APA, 2013), in which clinical supervisors are urged to continue in-person supervision when possible, be reasonably proficient in the technologies they are using, and consult with knowledgeable others to reduce the risks that come with ongoing technological advancements. These are daunting but necessary steps, and they will more routinely become a part of the supervisor's mandate going forward.

On the more personal level, supervisors and their trainees will need to reach agreements about how they will communicate in cases of emergent clinical situations outside the supervisory hour (e.g., Will they use text messaging?). There is also the question of how distance supervision will affect the quality of the trainee's learning experience in supervision. Fortunately, the data on this issue are promising in that several studies have suggested that *cybersupervision* is as effective as individual face-to-face supervision and that both supervisors and supervisees have perceived no significant differences in their perceptions of the quality of the supervisory relationship (see Inman et al., 2014, for an overview).

FINAL REMARKS

In conclusion, whether CBS is conducted long distance or in person, individually or in groups, within a homogeneous cultural milieu or cross culturally, as part of clinical trials or routine clinical training, in the context of early professional development or continuing education, or between supervisor and supervisee or metasupervisor and supervisor, the field clearly has turned a corner. Long gone are the days when CBS was an afterthought in training, taken for granted as a naturally acquired competency, unmeasured and untested in research, and generally underrepresented in the literature. Now there is a growing body of empirical research on CBS to go along with the welcome appearance of professional standards, manuals, books, and scoring codes with which to understand and further develop this critical area of our profession.

We hope that this concise handbook has served as a convenient, elucidating reference for anyone who wishes to conduct CBS. As clinical psychologists who have spent (and continue to spend) a significant part of our careers involved in the direct training and supervision of CBT therapists, we know firsthand how rewarding it is to play a role in the development of our supervisees as they learn to bring the power and promise of evidenced-based CBT methods to their clients, present and future. We wish you all the best in your careers as you do the same.

Suggested Readings

Bennett-Levy, J., Thwaites, R., Haarhoff, B., & Perry, H. (2015). *Experiencing CBT from the inside out: A self-practice/self-reflection workbook for therapists.* New York, NY: Guilford.
Provides an excellent program of self-application of cognitive–behavioral therapy (CBT) for practitioners. A great resource for the learning of self-reflection, and the practicing of clinician self-care.

Corrie, S., & Lane, D. A. (2015). *CBT supervision.* London, United Kingdom: Sage.
Allows readers from the United States to get a sense of the delivery of CBT supervision and treatment from the British socio-political-economic system, thus bringing the issue of context to the fore.

Milne, D. (2009). *Evidence-based clinical supervision: Principles and practice.* Oxford, United Kingdom: Wiley-Blackwell.
From one of the leaders in empirical modeling and testing of mental health supervision, this text helps the reader appreciate how supervision is being advanced via rigorous research.

Newman, C. F. (2012). *Core competencies in cognitive–behavioral therapy: Becoming a highly effective and competent cognitive–behavioral therapist.* New York, NY: Routledge.
Spells out the knowledge, attitudes, and skills required to deliver top-quality CBT, including many supervision principles and illustrative vignettes in imparting these competencies to trainees in CBT.

Newman, C. F. (2013). Training cognitive behavioral therapy supervisors: Didactics, simulated practice, and "meta-supervision." *Journal of Cognitive Psychotherapy, 27,* 5–18.

Describes a graduate-level seminar in CBT supervision, as well as an extended vignette of cross-cultural metasupervision, which supplements the summaries of these topics within the body of the Newman and Kaplan text.

Sudak, D. M., Codd, R. T., Ludgate, J., Sokol, L., Fox, M. G., Reiser, R., & Milne, D. L. (2015). *Teaching and supervising cognitive–behavioral therapy.* Hoboken, NJ: Wiley.

The lead author is one of the top CBT psychiatrists in the world, thus giving the reader a prime example of how CBT supervision is applied in an interdisciplinary way.

Watkins, C. E., & Milne, D. L. (Eds.). (2014). *The Wiley international handbook of clinical supervision.* Chichester, West Sussex, United Kingdom: Wiley Blackwell.

Encyclopedic in its coverage, this magnum opus covers almost every conceivable special angle on the topic of clinical supervision across theoretical orientations. A comprehensive reference, with writings by top contributors from around the globe.

References

Accreditation Council for Graduate Medical Education. (2001). *Graduate medical education directory, 2001–2002.* Chicago, IL: American Medical Association.

Accreditation Council for Graduate Medical Education. (2014). The Psychiatry Milestone Project: A joint initiative of the Accreditation Council for Graduate Medical Education and the American Board of Psychiatry and Neurology. *Journal of Graduate Medical Education, 6*(suppl. 1), 284–304. http://dx.doi.org/10.4300/JGME-06-01s1-11

American Psychological Association. (2002). Ethical principles of psychologists and code of conduct. *American Psychologist, 57,* 1060–1073. http://dx.doi.org/10.1037/0003-066X.57.12.1060

American Psychological Association. (2010). *Ethical principles of psychologists and code of conduct (2002, Amended June 1, 2010).* Retrieved from http://www.apa.org/ethics/code/

American Psychological Association. (2013). Guidelines for the practice of telepsychology: Joint task force for the development of telepsychology guidelines for psychologists. *American Psychologist, 68,* 791–800.

American Psychological Association and Commission on Accreditation. (2009). Accredited internship and postdoctoral programs for training in psychology. *American Psychologist, 64,* 891–916. http://dx.doi.org/10.1037/a0017728

Ancis, J. R., & Ladany, N. (2010). A multicultural framework for counselor supervision. In N. Ladany & L. J. Bradley (Eds.), *Counsellor supervision* (pp. 53–95). New York, NY: Routledge.

Armstrong, P. V., & Freeston, M. H. (2006). Conceptualising and formulating cognitive therapy supervision. In N. Tarrier (Ed.), *Case formulation in cognitive–behaviour therapy* (pp. 349–371). New York, NY: Brunner-Routledge.

Bambling, M., King, R., Raue, P., Schweitzer, R., & Lambert, W. (2006). Clinical supervision: Its influence on client-related working alliance and client symptom reduction in the brief treatment of major depression. *Psychotherapy Research, 16*, 317–331. http://dx.doi.org/10.1080/10503300500268524

Bandura, A. B. (1986). *Social foundations of thought and action: A social cognitive theory.* Englewood, NJ: Prentice Hall.

Barlow, D. H., Ellard, K. K., Fairholme, C. P., Farchione, T. J., Boisseau, C. L., Allen, L. B., & Ehrenriech-May, J. T. (2011). *Unified protocol for transdiagnostic treatment of emotional disorders.* New York, NY: Oxford University Press.

Barton, S. (2015, July). Supervisory supervision—Conceptual model and practical guidance. Paper presented at the annual conference of the British Association for Behavioural and Cognitive Psychotherapies, Warwick, United Kingdom.

Beck, A. T. (1976). *Cognitive therapy and the emotional disorders.* New York, NY: International Universities Press.

Beck, A. T., Kovacs, M., & Weissman, A. (1979). Assessment of suicidal intention: The scale for suicide ideation. *Journal of Consulting and Clinical Psychology, 47*, 343–352. http://dx.doi.org/10.1037/0022-006X.47.2.343

Beck, A. T., Rush, A. J., Shaw, B., & Emery, G. (1979). *Cognitive therapy of depression.* New York, NY: Guilford.

Beck, A. T., Steer, R. A., & Brown, G. K. (1996). *Manual for the Beck Depression Inventory II.* San Antonio, TX: Psychological Corporation.

Beck, A. T., Wright, F. D., Newman, C. F., & Liese, B. S. (1993). *Cognitive therapy of substance abuse.* New York, NY: Guilford.

Beck, J. S. (2011). *Cognitive behavior therapy: Basics and beyond* (2nd ed.). New York, NY: Guilford.

Beidas, R. S., & Kendall, P. C. (2010). Training therapists in evidence-based practice: A critical review of studies from a systems-contextual perspective. *Clinical Psychology: Science and Practice, 17*, 1–30. http://dx.doi.org/10.1111/j.1468-2850.2009.01187.x

Beinart, H. (2014). Building and sustaining the supervisory relationship. In C. E. Watkins & D. L. Milne (Eds.), *The Wiley international handbook of clinical supervision* (pp. 255–281). Chichester, West Sussex, United Kingdom: Wiley Blackwell. http://dx.doi.org/10.1002/9781118846360.ch11

Belar, C. (2008). Supervisory issues in clinical health psychology. In C. A. Falender & E. P. Shafranske (Eds.), *Casebook for clinical supervision: A competency-based approach* (pp. 197–209). Washington, DC: American Psychological Association. http://dx.doi.org/10.1037/11792-010

Bennett-Levy, J. (2006). Therapist skills: A cognitive model of their acquisition and refinement. *Behavioural and Cognitive Psychotherapy, 34*, 57–78. http://dx.doi.org/10.1017/S1352465805002420

Bennett-Levy, J., McManus, F., Westling, B. E., & Fennell, M. (2009). Acquiring and refining CBT skills and competencies: Which training methods are perceived to be most effective? *Behavioural and Cognitive Psychotherapy, 37*, 571–583. http://dx.doi.org/10.1017/S1352465809990270

Bennett-Levy, J., & Padesky, C. A. (2014). Use it or lose it: Post-workshop reflection enhances learning and utilization of CBT skills. *Cognitive and Behavioral Practice, 21*, 12–19. http://dx.doi.org/10.1016/j.cbpra.2013.05.001

Bennett-Levy, J., Thwaites, R., Haarhoff, B., & Perry, H. (2015). *Experiencing CBT from the inside out: A self-practice/self-reflection workbook for therapists.* New York, NY: Guilford.

Bernard, J. M., & Goodyear, R. K. (2014). *Fundamentals of clinical supervision* (5th ed.). Upper Saddle River, NJ: Pearson.

Blackburn, I. M., James, I. A., Milne, D. L., Baker, C., Standart, S., Garland, A., & Reichelt, K. (2001). The revised cognitive therapy scale (CTS-R): Psychometric properties. *Behavioural and Cognitive Psychotherapy, 29*, 431–446. http://dx.doi.org/10.1017/S1352465801004040

Brown, L. A., Craske, M. G., Glenn, D. E., Stein, M. B., Sullivan, G., Sherbourne, C., . . . Rose, R. D. (2013). CBT competence in novice therapists improves anxiety outcomes. *Depression and Anxiety, 30*, 97–115. http://dx.doi.org/10.1002/da.22027

Burns, D. D. (1999). *The feeling good handbook.* New York, NY: Penguin Books.

Burns, D. D., & Spangler, D. L. (2000). Does psychotherapy homework lead to improvements in depression in cognitive–behavioral therapy or does improvement lead to increased homework compliance? *Journal of Consulting and Clinical Psychology, 68*, 46–56. http://dx.doi.org/10.1037/0022-006X.68.1.46

Calhoun, K. S., Moras, K., Pilkonis, P. A., & Rehm, L. P. (1998). Empirically supported treatments: Implications for training. *Journal of Consulting and Clinical Psychology, 66*, 151–162. http://dx.doi.org/10.1037/0022-006X.66.1.151

Campbell, J. M. (2005). *Essentials of clinical supervision.* Hoboken, NJ: Wiley.

Castro, F. G., Barrera, M., Jr., & Holleran Steiker, L. K. (2010). Issues and challenges in the design of culturally adapted evidence-based interventions. *Annual Review of Clinical Psychology, 6*, 213–239. http://dx.doi.org/10.1146/annurev-clinpsy-033109-132032

Corrie, S., & Lane, D. A. (2015). *CBT supervision.* London, United Kingdom: Sage.

Corrie, S., & Worrell, M. (2012). *The supervisor evaluation scale.* Unpublished instrument. Available from sarah.corrie@nhs.net.

Council of National Psychological Associations for the Advancement of Ethnic Minority Interests. (2009). *Psychology education and training from culture-specific and multiracial perspectives: Critical issues and recommendations.* Washington, DC: American Psychological Association.

Cummings, J. A., Ballantyne, E. C., & Scallion, L. M. (2015). Essential processes for cognitive behavioral clinical supervision: Agenda setting, problem-solving, and formative feedback. *Psychotherapy, 52*, 158–163. http://dx.doi.org/10.1037/a0038712

Davis, D. D. (2008). *Terminating therapy: A professional guide to ending therapy on a positive note*. Hoboken, NJ: Wiley.

DeLeire, T. (2000). The wage and employment effects of the Americans with Disabilities Act. *The Journal of Human Resources, 35*, 693–715. http://dx.doi.org/10.2307/146368

Dobson, D., & Dobson, K. S. (2009). *Evidence-based practice of cognitive–behavioral therapy*. New York, NY: Guilford.

Dryden, W., & Thorne, B. (Eds.). (1991). *Training and supervision for counselling in action*. London, United Kingdom: Sage.

Dunn, R., Callahan, J. L., Swift, J. K., & Ivanovic, M. (2013). Effects of pre-session centering for therapists on session presence and effectiveness. *Psychotherapy Research, 23*, 78–85. http://dx.doi.org/10.1080/10503307.2012.731713

Edwards, D. (2010). Play and metaphor in clinical supervision: Keeping creativity alive. *The Arts in Psychotherapy, 37*, 248–254. http://dx.doi.org/10.1016/j.aip.2010.04.011

Eells, T. D. (2011). What is an evidence-based psychotherapy case formulation? *Psychotherapy Bulletin, 46*, 17–21.

Fadiman, A. (1997). *The spirit catches you and you fall down*. New York, NY: Farrar, Straus, & Giroux.

Falender, C. A., & Shafranske, E. P. (in press). *Supervision essentials for a competency-based model*. Washington, DC: American Psychological Association.

Falender, C. A., & Shafranske, E. P. (2004). *Clinical supervision: A competency-based approach*. Washington, DC: American Psychological Association. http://dx.doi.org/10.1037/10806-000

Falender, C. A., & Shafranske, E. P. (2007). Competence in competency-based supervision practice: Construct and application. *Professional Psychology: Research and Practice, 38*, 232–240. http://dx.doi.org/10.1037/0735-7028.38.3.232

Falender, C. A., & Shafranske, E. P. (Eds.). (2008). *Casebook for clinical supervision: A competency-based approach*. Washington, DC: American Psychological Association. http://dx.doi.org/10.1037/11792-000

Falender, C. A., & Shafranske, E. P. (2012). *Getting the most out of clinical training and supervision: A guide for practicum students and interns*. Washington, DC: American Psychological Association.

Falender, C. A., Shafranske, E. P., & Falicov, C. J. (Eds.). (2014). *Multiculturalism and diversity in clinical supervision: A competency-based approach.* Washington, DC: American Psychological Association.

Fleming, I., Gone, R., Diver, A., & Fowler, B. (2007). Risk supervision in Rochdale. *Clinical Psychology Forum, 176,* 22–25.

Fleming, I., & Steen, L. (2012). *Supervision and clinical psychology: Theory, practice, and perspectives.* London, United Kingdom: Routledge.

Fouad, N. A., Grus, C. L., Hatcher, R. L., Kaslow, N. J., Hutchings, P. S., Madson, M. B., . . . Crossman, R. E. (2009). Competency benchmarks: A model for understanding and measuring competence in professional psychology across training levels. *Training and Education in Professional Psychology, 3*(4, Suppl), S5–S26. http://dx.doi.org/10.1037/a0015832

Frankl, V. (1959). *Man's search for meaning.* New York, NY: Washington Square Press.

Friedberg, R. D., Gorman, A. A., & Beidel, D. C. (2009). Training psychologists for cognitive–behavioral therapy in the raw world: A rubric for supervisors. *Behavior Modification, 33,* 104–123. http://dx.doi.org/10.1177/0145445508322609

Friedberg, R. D., Mahr, S., & Mahr, F. (2010). Training psychiatrists in cognitive behavioral therapy: Current status and horizons. *Current Psychiatry Reviews, 6,* 159–170. http://dx.doi.org/10.2174/157340010791792563

Ginzburg, D. M., Bohn, C., Höfling, V., Weck, F., Clark, D. M., & Stangier, U. (2012). Treatment specific competence predicts outcome in cognitive therapy for social anxiety disorder. *Behaviour Research and Therapy, 50,* 747–752. http://dx.doi.org/10.1016/j.brat.2012.09.001

Greenberger, D., & Padesky, C. (2015). *Mind over mood* (2nd ed.). New York, NY: Guilford.

Griner, D., & Smith, T. B. (2006). Culturally adapted mental health intervention: A meta-analytic review. *Psychotherapy: Theory, Research, Practice, Training, 43,* 531–548. http://dx.doi.org/10.1037/0033-3204.43.4.531

Hawkins, P., & Shohet, R. (2012). *Supervision in the helping professions* (4th ed.). Maidenhead, Berkshire, United Kingdom: Open University Press.

Hayes, S. C., Strosahl, K. D., & Wilson, K. G. (1999). *Acceptance and commitment therapy: An experiential approach to behavior change.* New York, NY: Guilford.

Hays, P. A., & Iwamasa, G. Y. (Eds.). (2006). *Culturally responsive cognitive–behavioral therapy: Assessment, practice, and supervision.* Washington, DC: American Psychological Association. http://dx.doi.org/10.1037/11433-000

Hipple, J., & Beamish, P. M. (2007). Supervision of counselor trainees with clients in crisis. *Journal of Professional Counseling: Practice, Theory, & Research, 35,* 1–16.

Huey, S. J., Jr., & Polo, A. J. (2008). Evidence-based psychosocial treatments for ethnic minority youth. *Journal of Clinical Child and Adolescent Psychology, 37,* 262–301. http://dx.doi.org/10.1080/15374410701820174

Inman, A. G. (2006). Supervisor multicultural competence and its relation to supervisory process and outcome. *Journal of Marital and Family Therapy, 32,* 73–85. http://dx.doi.org/10.1111/j.1752-0606.2006.tb01589.x

Inman, A. G., Hutman, H., Pendse, A., Devdas, L., Luu, L., & Ellis, M. V. (2014). Current trends concerning supervisors, supervisees, and clients in clinical supervision. In C. E. Watkins & D. L. Milne (Eds.), *The Wiley international handbook of clinical supervision* (pp. 61–102). Chichester, West Sussex, United Kingdom: Wiley Blackwell. http://dx.doi.org/10.1002/9781118846360.ch4

Iwamasa, G. Y., Pai, S. M., & Sorocco, K. H. (2006). Multicultural cognitive–behavioral therapy supervision. In P. A. Hays & G. Y. Iwamasa (Eds.), *Culturally responsive cognitive–behavioral therapy: Assessment, practice, and supervision* (pp. 267–281). Washington, DC: American Psychological Association. http://dx.doi.org/10.1037/11433-012

Jamison, K. R. (1995). *An unquiet mind: A memoir of moods and madness.* New York, NY: Vintage Books.

Jarrett, R. B., Vittengl, J. R., Clark, L. A., & Thase, M. E. (2011). Skills of Cognitive Therapy (SoCT): A new measure of patients' comprehension and use. *Psychological Assessment, 23,* 578–586. http://dx.doi.org/10.1037/a0022485

Joint Task Force for the Development of Telepsychology Guidelines for Psychologists. (2013). Guidelines for the practice of telepsychology. *American Psychologist, 68,* 791–800. http://dx.doi.org/10.1037/a0035001

Kamholz, B. W., Liverant, G. I., Black, S., Aaronson, C. J., & Hill, J. (2014). Beyond psychologist training: CBT education for psychiatry residents. *The Behavior Therapist, 37,* 218–226.

Kaslow, N. J., & Bell, K. D. (2008). A competency-based approach to supervision. In C. A. Falender & E. P. Shafranske (Eds.), *Clinical casebook for clinical supervision: A competency-based approach* (pp. 17–38). Washington, DC: American Psychological Association. http://dx.doi.org/10.1037/11792-002

Kaslow, N. J., Borden, K. A., Collins, F. L., Jr., Forrest, L., Illfelder-Kaye, J., Nelson, P. D., . . . Willmuth, M. E. (2004). Competencies conference: Future directions in education and credentialing in professional psychology. *Journal of Clinical Psychology, 60*(7), 699–712. http://dx.doi.org/10.1002/jclp.20016

Kaslow, N. J., Rubin, N. J., Forrest, L., Elman, N. S., Van Horne, B. A., Jacobs, S. C., . . . Thorn, B. E. (2007). Recognizing, assessing, and intervening with problems of professional competence. *Professional Psychology: Research and Practice, 38,* 479–492. http://dx.doi.org/10.1037/0735-7028.38.5.479

Kazantzis, N., Whittington, C., & Dattilio, F. (2010). Meta-analysis of homework effects in cognitive and behavioral therapy: A replication and extension. *Clinical Psychology: Science and Practice, 17,* 144–156. http://dx.doi.org/10.1111/j.1468-2850.2010.01204.x

Kendall, P. C., Gosch, E., Furr, J. M., & Sood, E. (2008). Flexibility within fidelity. *Journal of the American Academy of Child and Adolescent Psychiatry, 47*, 987–993. http://dx.doi.org/10.1097/CHI.0b013e31817eed2f

Koocher, G. P., Shafranske, E. P., & Falender, C. A. (2008). Addressing ethical and legal issues in clinical supervision. In C. A. Falender & E. P. Shafranske (Eds.), *Casebook for clinical supervision: A competency-based approach* (pp. 159–180). Washington, DC: American Psychological Association. http://dx.doi.org/ 10.1037/11792-008

Kroenke, K., Spitzer, R. L., & Williams, J. B. W. (2001). The PHQ-9: Validity of a brief depression severity measure. *Journal of General Internal Medicine, 16*, 606–613. http://dx.doi.org/10.1046/j.1525-1497.2001.016009606.x

Kuyken, W., Padesky, C. A., & Dudley, R. (2009). *Collaborative case conceptualization: Working effectively with clients in cognitive-behavioral therapy.* New York, NY: Guilford.

Kuyken, W., & Tsivrikos, D. (2009). Therapist competence, comorbidity and cognitive–behavioral therapy for depression. *Psychotherapy and Psychosomatics, 78*, 42–48. http://dx.doi.org/10.1159/000172619

Ladany, N. (2004). Psychotherapy supervision: What lies beneath. *Psychotherapy Research, 14*, 1–19.

Ladany, N., Friedlander, M. L., & Nelson, M. L. (2005). *Critical events in psychotherapy supervision: An interpersonal approach.* Washington, DC: American Psychological Association. http://dx.doi.org/10.1037/10958-000

Ladany, N., Hill, C. E., Corbett, M. M., & Nutt, E. A. (1996). Nature, extent, and importance of what psychotherapy trainees do not disclose to their supervisors. *Journal of Counseling Psychology, 43*, 10–24. http://dx.doi.org/10.1037/ 0022-0167.43.1.10

Ladany, N., Lehrman-Waterman, D., Molinaro, M., & Wolgast, B. (1999). Psychotherapy supervisor ethical practices: Adherence to guidelines, supervisory working alliance, and supervisee satisfaction. *The Counseling Psychologist, 27*, 443–475. http://dx.doi.org/10.1177/0011000099273008

Lambert, M. J., Lunnen, K., Umphress, V., Hansen, N., & Burlingame, G. M. (1994). *Administration and scoring manual for the Outcome Questionnaire (OQ-45.1).* Salt Lake City, UT: IHC Center for Behavioral Healthcare Efficacy.

Leahy, R. L. (2003). *Cognitive therapy techniques: A practitioner's guide.* New York, NY: Guilford.

Leahy, R. L., Holland, S. J., & McGinn, L. (2011). *Treatment plans and interventions for depression and anxiety disorders: The clinician's toolbox* (2nd ed.). New York, NY: Guilford.

Ledley, D. R., Marx, B. P., & Heimberg, R. H. (2010). *Making cognitive–behavioral therapy work: Clinical process for new practitioners* (2nd ed.). New York, NY: Guilford.

Liese, B. S., & Beck, J. S. (1997). Cognitive therapy supervision. In C. E. Watkins (Ed.), *Handbook of psychotherapy supervision* (pp. 114–133). New York, NY: Wiley.

Livni, D., Crowe, T. P., & Gonsalvez, C. J. (2012). Effects of supervision modality and intensity on alliance and outcomes for the supervisee. *Rehabilitation Psychology, 57,* 178–186. http://dx.doi.org/10.1037/a0027452

Mannix, K. A., Blackburn, I. M., Garland, A., Gracie, J., Moorey, S., Reid, B., . . . Scott, J. (2006). Effectiveness of brief training in cognitive behaviour therapy techniques for palliative care practitioners. *Palliative Medicine, 20,* 579–584. http://dx.doi.org/10.1177/0269216306071058

McManus, F., Rakovshik, S., Kennerley, H., Fennell, M., & Westbrook, D. (2012). An investigation of the accuracy of therapists' self-assessment of cognitive–behaviour therapy skills. *British Journal of Clinical Psychology, 51,* 292–306. http://dx.doi.org/10.1111/j.2044-8260.2011.02028.x

McNeill, B., & Stoltenberg, C. (2016). *Supervision essentials for the integrative developmental model.* Washington, DC: American Psychological Association.

Miller, W. R., Yahne, C. E., Moyers, T. B., Martinez, J., & Pirritano, M. (2004). A randomized trial of methods to help clinicians learn motivational interviewing. *Journal of Consulting and Clinical Psychology, 72,* 1050–1062. http://dx.doi.org/10.1037/0022-006X.72.6.1050

Milne, D. (2007). An empirical definition of clinical supervision. *British Journal of Clinical Psychology, 46,* 437–447. http://dx.doi.org/10.1348/014466507X197415

Milne, D. L. (2009). *Evidence-based clinical supervision: Principles and practice.* Oxford, United Kingdom: Wiley-Blackwell.

Milne, D. L. (2014). Toward an evidence-based approach to clinical supervision. In C. E. Watkins & D. L. Milne (Eds.), *The Wiley international handbook of clinical supervision* (pp. 38–60). Chichester, West Sussex, United Kingdom: Wiley Blackwell. http://dx.doi.org/10.1002/9781118846360.ch3

Milne, D. L., Aylott, H., Fitzpatrick, H., & Ellis, M. V. (2008). How does clinical supervision work? Using a "best evidence synthesis" approach to construct a basic model of supervision. *The Clinical Supervisor, 27,* 170–190. http://dx.doi.org/10.1080/07325220802487915

Milne, D. L., & Dunkerley, C. (2010). Towards evidence-based clinical supervision: The development and evaluation of four CBT guidelines. *The Cognitive Behaviour Therapist, 3,* 43–57. http://dx.doi.org/10.1017/S1754470X10000048

Milne, D. L., Pilkington, J., Gracie, J., & James, I. A. (2003). Transferring skills from supervision to therapy. A qualitative N = 1 analysis. *Behavioural and Cognitive Psychotherapy, 31,* 193–202. http://dx.doi.org/10.1017/S1352465803002078

Milne, D. L., & Reiser, R. (2011). Observing competence in CBT supervision: A systematic review of the available instruments. *The Cognitive Behaviour Therapist, 4*, 89–100. http://dx.doi.org/10.1017/S1754470X11000067

Milne, D. L., & Reiser, R. (2014). SAGE: A scale for rating competence in CBT supervision. In C. E. Watkins & D. L. Milne (Eds.), *The Wiley international handbook of clinical supervision* (pp. 402–415). Chichester, West Sussex, United Kingdom: Wiley Blackwell. http://dx.doi.org/10.1002/9781118846360.ch18

Milne, D. L., Reiser, R., Aylott, H., Dunkerley, C., Fitzpatrick, H., & Wharton, S. (2010). The systematic review as an empirical approach to improving CBT supervision. *International Journal of Cognitive Therapy, 3*, 278–294. http://dx.doi.org/10.1521/ijct.2010.3.3.278

Milne, D. L., Reiser, R. P., Cliffe, T., & Raine, R. (2011). SAGE: Preliminary evaluation of an instrument for observing competence in CBT supervision. *The Cognitive Behaviour Therapist, 4*, 123–138. http://dx.doi.org/10.1017/S1754470X11000079

Milne, D. L., Sheikh, A. I., Pattison, S., & Wilkinson, A. (2011). Evidence-based training for clinical supervisors: A systematic review of 11 controlled studies. *The Clinical Supervisor, 30*, 53–71. http://dx.doi.org/10.1080/07325223.2011.564955

Murphy, M. J., & Wright, D. W. (2005). Supervisees' perspectives of power use in supervision. *Journal of Marital and Family Therapy, 31*, 283–295. http://dx.doi.org/10.1111/j.1752-0606.2005.tb01569.x

Muse, K., & McManus, F. (2013). A systematic review of methods for assessing competence in cognitive–behavioural therapy. *Clinical Psychology Review, 33*, 484–499. http://dx.doi.org/10.1016/j.cpr.2013.01.010

Needleman, L. (1999). *Cognitive case conceptualization: A guide for practitioners.* Mahwah, NJ: Lawrence Erlbaum Associates.

Nelson, M. L. (2014). Using the major formats of clinical supervision. In C. E. Watkins & D. L. Milne (Eds.), *The Wiley international handbook of clinical supervision* (pp. 308–328). Chichester, West Sussex, United Kingdom: Wiley Blackwell. http://dx.doi.org/10.1002/9781118846360.ch13

Nelson, M. L., Barnes, K. L., Evans, A. L., & Triggiano, P. J. (2008). Working with conflict in clinical supervision: Wise supervisors' perspectives. *Journal of Counseling Psychology, 55*, 172–184. http://dx.doi.org/10.1037/0022-0167.55.2.172

Newman, C. F. (1998). Therapeutic and supervisory relationships in cognitive–behavioral therapies: Similarities and differences. *Journal of Cognitive Psychotherapy, 12*, 95–108.

Newman, C. F. (2010). Competency in conducting cognitive–behavioral therapy: Foundational, functional, and supervisory aspects. *Psychotherapy: Theory, Research, Practice, Training, 47*, 12–19. http://dx.doi.org/10.1037/a0018849

Newman, C. F. (2012). *Core competencies in cognitive–behavioral therapy: Becoming a highly effective and competent cognitive–behavioral therapist.* New York, NY: Routledge.

Newman, C. F. (2013). Training cognitive behavioral therapy supervisors: Didactics, simulated practice, and "meta-supervision." *Journal of Cognitive Psychotherapy, 27,* 5–18. http://dx.doi.org/10.1891/0889-8391.27.1.5

Newman, C. F. (2015, June). *Becoming a virtuoso in CBT: Learning and interpreting the "score" with technique and artistry.* Paper delivered at the annual conference of the British Association for Behavioural and Cognitive Psychotherapies, Warwick, United Kingdom.

Newman, C. F., & Beck, J. S. (2008). Selecting, training, and supervising therapists in randomized controlled trials. In A. M. Nezu & C. M. Nezu (Eds.), *Evidence-based outcome research: A practical guide to conducting randomized controlled trials for psychosocial interventions* (pp. 245–262). Oxford, United Kingdom: Oxford University Press.

Norcross, J. C., & Lambert, M. J. (2011). Psychotherapy relationships that work II. *Psychotherapy, 48,* 4–8. http://dx.doi.org/10.1037/a0022180

O'Donohue, W. T., & Fisher, J. E. (Eds.). (2009). *General principles and empirically supported techniques of cognitive–behavior therapy.* Hoboken, NJ: Wiley.

Padesky, C. A. (1996). Developing cognitive therapist competency: Teaching and supervision models. In P. M. Salkovskis (Ed.), *Frontiers of cognitive therapy* (pp. 261–292). New York, NY: Guilford.

Patel, N. (2004). Difference and power in supervision: The case of culture and racism. In I. Fleming & L. Steen (Eds.), *Supervision and clinical psychology: Theory, practice, and perspectives* (pp. 108–134). Hove, East Sussex, United Kingdom: Brunner-Routledge.

Persons, J. (2008). *The case formulation approach to cognitive–behavior therapy.* New York, NY: Guilford.

Phelps, D. L. (2011). Supervisee experiences of corrective feedback in clinical supervision. *Psychotherapy Bulletin, 46,* 14–18.

Pilling, S., & Roth, A. D. (2014). The competent clinical supervisor. In C. E. Watkins & D. L. Milne (Eds.), *The Wiley international handbook of clinical supervision* (pp. 20–37). Chichester, West Sussex, United Kingdom: Wiley Blackwell. http://dx.doi.org/10.1002/9781118846360.ch2

Pope, K. S., & Vasquez, M. J. T. (2011). *Ethics in psychotherapy and counseling: A practical guide.* Hoboken, NJ: Wiley. http://dx.doi.org/10.1002/9781118001875

Rakovshik, S. (2015, July). *The Supervisor Competence Scale: Development and psychometric properties.* Paper presented at the annual conference of the British Association for Behavioural and Cognitive Psychotherapies, Warwick, United Kingdom.

Rakovshik, S. G., & McManus, F. (2010). Establishing evidence-based training in cognitive behavioral therapy: A review of current empirical findings and theoretical guidance. *Clinical Psychology Review, 30*, 496–516. http://dx.doi.org/10.1016/j.cpr.2010.03.004

Rees, C. S., McEvoy, P., & Nathan, P. R. (2005). Relationship between homework completion and outcome in cognitive behaviour therapy. *Cognitive Behaviour Therapy, 34*, 242–247. http://dx.doi.org/10.1080/16506070510011548

Reiser, R. P. (2014). Supervising cognitive and behavioural therapies. In C. E. Watkins & D. L. Milne (Eds.), *The Wiley international handbook of clinical supervision* (pp. 493–517). Chichester, West Sussex, United Kingdom: Wiley Blackwell. http://dx.doi.org/10.1002/9781118846360.ch24

Reiser, R. P., & Milne, D. (2012). Supervising cognitive-behavioral psychotherapy: Pressing needs, impressing possibilities. *Journal of Contemporary Psychotherapy, 42*, 161–171. http://dx.doi.org/10.1007/s10879-011-9200-6

Reiser, R. P., & Milne, D. L. (2014). A systematic review and reformulation of outcome evaluation in clinical supervision: Applying the fidelity framework. *Training and Education in Professional Psychology, 8*, 149–157. http://dx.doi.org/10.1037/tep0000031

Rodolfa, E., Bent, R., Eisman, E., Nelson, P., Rehm, L., & Ritchie, P. (2005). A cube model for competency development: Implications for psychology educators and regulators. *Professional Psychology: Research and Practice, 36*, 347–354. http://dx.doi.org/10.1037/0735-7028.36.4.347

Ronen, T., & Rosenbaum, M. (1998). Beyond direct verbal instructions in cognitive behavioral supervision. *Cognitive and Behavioral Practice, 5*, 7–23.

Roth, A. D., & Pilling, S. (2007). *The competences required to deliver effective cognitive and behavioural therapy for people with depression and with anxiety disorders.* London, England: Department of Health.

Roth, A. D., & Pilling, S. (2008a). *The Competence Framework for Supervision.* Retrieved from http://www.ucl.ac.uk/clinical-psychology/CORE/supervision_framework.htm

Roth, A. D., & Pilling, S. (2008b). Using an evidence-based methodology to identify the competencies required to deliver effective cognitive and behavioural therapy for depression and anxiety disorders. *Behavioural and Cognitive Psychotherapy, 36*, 129–147. http://dx.doi.org/10.1017/S1352465808004141

Rousmaniere, T. (2014). Using technology to enhance clinical supervision and training. In C. E. Watkins & D. L. Milne (Eds.), *The Wiley international handbook of clinical supervision* (pp. 204–237). Chichester, West Sussex, United Kingdom: Wiley Blackwell. http://dx.doi.org/10.1002/9781118846360.ch9

Safran, J. D., & Muran, J. C. (2001). A relational approach to training and supervision in cognitive psychotherapy. *Journal of Cognitive Psychotherapy, 15*, 3–16.

Scaife, J. (2001). *Supervising the reflective practitioner: An essential guide to theory and practice.* Hove, East Sussex, United Kingdom: Routledge.

Sholomskas, D. E., Syracuse-Siewert, G., Rounsaville, B. J., Ball, S. A., Nuro, K. F., & Carroll, K. M. (2005). We don't train in vain: A dissemination trial of three strategies of training clinicians in cognitive–behavioral therapy. *Journal of Consulting and Clinical Psychology, 73,* 106–115. http://dx.doi.org/10.1037/ 0022-006X.73.1.106

Simons, A. D., Padesky, C. A., Montemarano, J., Lewis, C. C., Murakami, J., Lamb, K., . . . Beck, A. T. (2010). Training and dissemination of cognitive behavior therapy for depression in adults: A preliminary examination of therapist competence and client outcomes. *Journal of Consulting and Clinical Psychology, 78,* 751–756. http://dx.doi.org/10.1037/a0020569

Stott, R., Mansell, W., Salkovskis, P., Lavender, A., & Cartwright-Hatton, S. (2010). *Oxford guide to metaphors in CBT.* Oxford, United Kingdom: Oxford University Press.

Strauss, J. L., Hayes, A. M., Johnson, S. L., Newman, C. F., Brown, G. K., Barber, J. P., . . . Beck, A. T. (2006). Early alliance, alliance ruptures, and symptom change in a nonrandomized trial of cognitive therapy for avoidant and obsessive-compulsive personality disorders. *Journal of Consulting and Clinical Psychology, 74,* 337–345. http://dx.doi.org/10.1037/0022-006X.74.2.337

Strunk, D. R., Brotman, M. A., DeRubeis, R. J., & Hollon, S. D. (2010). Therapist competence in cognitive therapy for depression: Predicting subsequent symptom change. *Journal of Consulting and Clinical Psychology, 78,* 429–437. http:// dx.doi.org/10.1037/a0019631

Strunk, D. R., DeRubeis, R. J., Chiu, A. W., & Alvarez, J. (2007). Patients' competence in and performance of cognitive therapy skills: Relation to the reduction of relapse risk following treatment for depression. *Journal of Consulting and Clinical Psychology, 75,* 523–530. http://dx.doi.org/10.1037/0022-006X.75.4.523

Sturmey, P. (Ed.). (2009). *Clinical case formulation: Varieties of approaches.* London, United Kingdom: Wiley-Blackwell. http://dx.doi.org/10.1002/9780470747513

Sudak, D. M. (2009). Training in cognitive behavioral therapy in psychiatry residency: An overview for educators. *Behavior Modification, 33,* 124–137. http:// dx.doi.org/10.1177/1059601108322626

Sudak, D. M., Beck, J. S., & Wright, J. (2003). Cognitive behavioral therapy: A blueprint for attaining and assessing psychiatry resident competency. *Academic Psychiatry, 27,* 154–159. http://dx.doi.org/10.1176/appi.ap.27.3.154

Sudak, D. M., Codd, R. T., Ludgate, J., Sokol, L., Fox, M. G., Reiser, R., & Milne, D. L. (2015). *Teaching and supervising cognitive–behavioral therapy.* Hoboken, NJ: Wiley.

Swift, J. K., Callahan, J. L., Rousmaniere, T. G., Whipple, J. L., Dexter, K., & Wrape, E. R. (2015). Using client outcome monitoring as a tool for supervision. *Psychotherapy*, *52*, 180–184. http://dx.doi.org/10.1037/a0037659

Tarrier, N. (Ed.). (2006). *Case formulation in cognitive–behavioral therapy: The treatment of challenging and complex cases*. New York, NY: Routledge/Taylor & Francis.

Thomas, J. T. (2007). Informed consent through contracting for supervision: Minimizing risks, enhancing benefits. *Professional Psychology: Research and Practice*, *38*, 221–231. http://dx.doi.org/10.1037/0735-7028.38.3.221

Thomas, J. T. (2014). International ethics for psychotherapy supervisors: Principles, practices, and future directions. In C. E. Watkins & D. L. Milne (Eds.), *The Wiley international handbook of clinical supervision* (pp. 131–154). Chichester, West Sussex, United Kingdom: Wiley Blackwell. http://dx.doi.org/10.1002/9781118846360.ch6

Trepka, C., Rees, A., Shapiro, D. A., Hardy, G. E., & Barkham, M. (2004). Therapist competence and outcome of cognitive therapy for depression. *Cognitive Therapy and Research*, *28*, 143–157. http://dx.doi.org/10.1023/B:COTR.0000021536.39173.66

Tsui, M., O'Donoghue, K., & Ng, A. K. T. (2014). Culturally competent and diversity-sensitive clinical supervision: An international perspective. In C. E. Watkins & D. L. Milne (Eds.), *The Wiley international handbook of clinical supervision* (pp. 238–254). Chichester, West Sussex, United Kingdom: Wiley Blackwell. http://dx.doi.org/10.1002/9781118846360.ch10

Waller, G. (2009). Evidence-based treatment and therapist drift. *Behaviour Research and Therapy*, *47*, 119–127. http://dx.doi.org/10.1016/j.brat.2008.10.018

Watkins, C. E., Jr. (Ed.). (1997). *Handbook of psychotherapy supervision*. Hoboken, NJ: Wiley.

Watkins, C. E., Jr. (2011). Psychotherapy supervision since 1909: Some friendly observations about its first century. *Journal of Contemporary Psychotherapy*, *41*, 57–67. http://dx.doi.org/10.1007/s10879-010-9152-2

Watkins, C. E., & Milne, D. L. (Eds.). (2014). *The Wiley international handbook of clinical supervision*. Chichester, West Sussex, United Kingdom: Wiley Blackwell. http://dx.doi.org/10.1002/9781118846360

Webb, C. A., DeRubeis, R. J., & Barber, J. P. (2010). Therapist adherence/competence and treatment outcome: A meta-analytic review. *Journal of Consulting and Clinical Psychology*, *78*, 200–211. http://dx.doi.org/10.1037/a0018912

Young, J., & Beck, A. T. (1980). *The Cognitive Therapy Rating Scale manual*. Unpublished manuscript. University of Pennsylvania. Retrieved from https://www.beckinstitute.org/wp-content/uploads/2015/10/CTRS-current-10-2011-Cognitive-Therapy-Rating-Scale-2.pdf

Index

About the Authors

Cory F. Newman, PhD, ABPP, is director of the Center for Cognitive Therapy, professor of psychology in psychiatry at the University of Pennsylvania Perelman School of Medicine, and adjunct faculty at the Beck Institute for Cognitive Behavior Therapy. He is a diplomate of the American Board of Professional Psychology, and a founding fellow of the Academy of Cognitive Therapy. He earned his doctorate in clinical psychology from the State University of New York at Stony Brook in 1987 and subsequently completed a postdoctoral fellowship at the Center for Cognitive Therapy under the mentorship of Dr. Aaron T. Beck. Since then, Dr. Newman has maintained a full caseload of clients and has supervised more than 300 postdoctoral fellows, psychiatry residents, predoctoral students, international Beck Scholars, and other mental healthcare practitioners. He has served as a protocol cognitive-behavioral therapist and supervisor on numerous large-scale psychotherapy outcome studies, including the Penn-Vanderbilt-Rush Treatment of Depression Projects and the NIDA Multisite Collaborative Study on Treatments for Cocaine Abuse. While on sabbatical at the University of Colorado at Boulder in fall 2011, Dr. Newman taught the graduate seminar on the fundamentals of cognitive–behavioral supervision.

Dr. Newman is an international lecturer, having presented more than 200 cognitive–behavioral therapy (CBT) workshops and seminars throughout the U.S., as well as in 18 other countries. He is the lead author of dozens of articles and chapters of CBT for a range of clinical problems and has authored or coauthored six books, including *Bipolar Disorder: A Cognitive Therapy Approach* and *Core Competencies in Cognitive–Behavioral Therapy: Becoming a Highly Effective and Competent Cognitive–Behavioral Therapist*. On the side, Dr. Newman is an avid hockey player and a trained classical pianist.

Danielle A. Kaplan, PhD, is the director of the Predoctoral Psychology Internship at New York University (NYU)-Bellevue Hospital Center, where she is a clinical assistant professor in the NYU School of Medicine's Department of Psychiatry. She also coordinates CBT training and supervision for the NYU psychiatry residency. Dr. Kaplan received her doctorate in clinical psychology from the University of North Carolina at Chapel Hill. Since then, she has practiced CBT in community mental health, hospital-based, and private-practice settings and has taught and supervised CBT at Northwestern University and Yeshiva University's Ferkauf Graduate School of Psychology. Dr. Kaplan is the author of numerous book chapters and conference presentations on topics, including diversity training, cross-cultural mental health issues, and vicarious traumatization. In addition to her teaching and supervisory responsibilities, she maintains a private psychotherapy practice where she specializes in CBT for depression and anxiety disorders and reproductive and perinatal mental health. Dr. Kaplan is an enthusiastic traveler, dancer, and student of other languages.